# A TASTE OF

# INDOCHINA

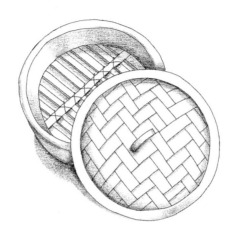

# A TASTE OF
# INDOCHINA

## JAN CASTORINA & DIMITRA STAIS

PHOTOGRAPHY BY ASHLEY MACKEVICIUS

STYLING BY MARIE HELENE CLAUZON

ILLUSTRATIONS BY SUE NINHAM

Hodder & Stoughton

FOOD EDITOR: ANNE MARSHALL

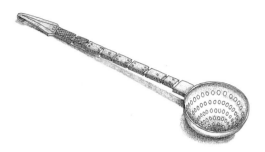

A Hodder & Stoughton Book

This edition published in 1995 by
Hodder Headline Australia Pty Limited
(a member of the Hodder Headline Group)
10–16 South Street, Rydalmere NSW 2116

National Library of Australia Cataloguing-in-Publication data

Castorina, Jan
    A Taste of Indochina

Includes index.
ISBN 0 7336 0120 0.

1. Cookery, Southeast Asian. I. Stais, Dimitra
II. Title.

641.5959

Printed in China

# *Con*

## A TASTE OF INDOCHINA
~ 6 ~

## THE HERBS AND SPICES OF INDOCHINA
~ 8 ~

## THE PANTRY GUIDE
~ 10 ~

## APPETISERS AND SNACKS
~ 14 ~

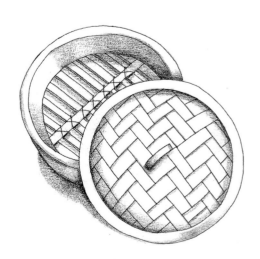

# tents

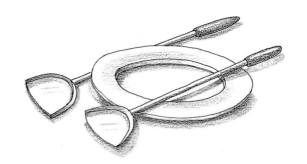

FLAVOUR-FILLED SOUPS

~ 32 ~

NOODLES AND RICE

~ 42 ~

MAIN COURSES

~ 64 ~

SALADS AND VEGETABLES

~ 126 ~

DESSERTS

~ 144 ~

THE ESSENTIALS

~ 154 ~

GLOSSARY

~ 156 ~

GUIDE TO MEASURES

~ 157 ~

INDEX

~ 158 ~

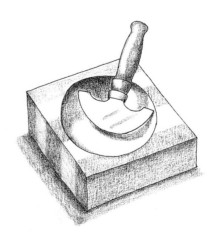

# A Taste of Indochina

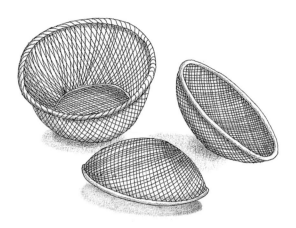

This book is an exploration of the flavours of Thailand, Vietnam, Laos and Cambodia.

The flavours of Thailand are varied and unique. In each region the food is prepared differently, sometimes subtly and sometimes quite remarkably.

In a Thai family meal there are several courses, all of which are served at the one time. A curry, a soup and a large bowl of steamed jasmine or sticky rice are the main features and are often served with a salad dish and a noodle dish. The soup is eaten first, during the meal or last.

Delicious sauces and condiments are served with the meal to add extra flavour and explosions of spice.

The Vietnamese, Laotian and Cambodian dishes are distinctively light and delicate in flavour with an abundant use of crisp raw vegetables to accompany every meal. What makes their foods so healthy is the many raw salads and vegetables they eat, and most cooked dishes are either steamed or stir-fried using minimal oil.

A typical meal in this part of Asia will consist of a soup, a noodle dish, a meat dish, a bowl of glutinous or steamed rice, an assorted vegetable platter and some fish dipping sauce and perhaps a separate bowl of chilli sauce to add spice to the meal.

The desserts from these countries are usually based on fresh fruits and coconut and are usually served at more formal dinners. Although sweets are often eaten as snacks during the day, as in Thailand where they are bought from street vendors.

# The Herbs and Spices of Indochina

Ground Cumin

Ground Turmeric

Galangal Powder

Five Spice Powder

Paprika

Black Pepper

Mint

Dried Galangal

Ground Coriander

Garlic

Ginger

Dried Kaffir Lime Leaves

Fresh Kaffir Lime Leaves

Coriander

Garlic Chives

Red and Green Chillies

Basil

Chilli Powder

Lemon Grass

# The Pantry Guide

There are a few ingredients you may not have heard of but they are easily obtainable from Asian food stores and some supermarkets. Most of the sauces and pastes will last for many months, once you have them they are always on hand to make delicious and simple dishes.

In the following pages there is a description of some of the unusual ingredients and a substitute where possible.

As these wonderful cuisines have become more and more popular, some thoughtful food manufacturers have gone to great lengths to make the ingredients a supermarket item. Ask at your favourite supermarket, you will be surprised what is available to you.

These are the essential ingredients that you will find described in detail within this Pantry Guide:

Bean Sauce

Chinese Dried Mushrooms

Curry Paste

Daikon Radish

Dried Shrimp

Egg Pastry

Fish Sauce

Gow Gees Pastry

Green Pawpaw (papaya)

Noodles

Oil

Oyster Sauce

Palm Sugar (gula jawa)

Pickled Mustard

Rice

Rice Paper

Rice Vinegar

Sambal Oelek

Sesame Oil

Shrimp Paste

Soy Sauce

Split Yellow Mung Beans

Spring Roll Wrappers

Sugar Cane

Sweet Chilli Sauce

Tamarind

Taro

Tofu, Firm or Hard
  (bean curd)

Wonton Wrappers

## Bean Sauce

This is a thick sauce made from soy beans. If unavailable you could substitute a little of the stronger flavoured black bean sauce.

## Chinese Dried Mushrooms

These are found in Asian food stores and some super-markets in plastic packets. Soak in hot water or stock for about 20 minutes until soft. The stem is removed then the mushroom sliced or left whole depending on the recipes. They have a strong flavour and are used sparingly. You can substitute fresh mushrooms but they do not have the same flavour.

## Curry Paste

Use good quality purchased or home-made curry pastes in the recipes. You can buy excellent red and green curry pastes from supermarkets as well as in Asian food stores. Any other varieties of curry pastes can also be found in Asian food stores.

## Daikon Radish

A long, thick, white, cylindrical vegetable that has a strong flavour. This radish is often used fresh to add flavour and a lovely crisp texture to salads.

## Dried Shrimp

Available in packets in Asian food stores. They have a strong fishy flavour and should be stored in the refrigerator, preferably in an airtight container.

## Egg Pastry

Available in Asian food stores in the refrigerator. It is found in rounds and squares and can be frozen for up to 2 months; thaw in the refrigerator.

## Fish Sauce

This is used throughout South-east Asia. It is made from small fish or prawns (shrimp) that are fermented. The sauce adds a burst of flavour to many dishes including sauces and condiments. It is found in supermarkets and Asian food stores.

## Gow Gees Pastry

Available in Asian food stores in the refrigerator. It is usually in 8cm (3in) rounds or squares and can be used for wontons and different appetiser recipes.

## Green Pawpaw (papaya)

This is the unripe red or yellow pawpaw (papaya), and is sliced finely or grated and used in a salad. The skin should be a bright green colour when unripe and the flesh pale and almost white. Ripe pawpaw cannot be used as a substitute.

## Noodles

**Bean Thread Vermicelli Noodles**
Use the noodles sold in 50g (1.75oz) packets. They are a white opaque colour when raw and after a soak in boiling water for 10 minutes become translucent and soft.
**Fresh Egg Noodles** These are found in the refrigerator in Asian food stores and come in very thin or thick noodles. They are also available in ribbons about 4mm (1/4in) wide. The noodles are made from wheat flour and egg and are used in a wide range of dishes. They are usually boiled for several minutes before using.

**Fresh Rice Noodles (banh pho)**
These are sold in sealed plastic packages near the counter or in the refrigerator in Asian food stores. They can be bought sliced or unsliced. The sliced version is in strips about 1cm (1/2in) wide. If you find the unsliced version, just cut slices from the block without unfolding it first. These noodles are also soaked in boiling water for about 10 minutes or so before using.
**Rice Stick Noodles** These noodles are thin long strips about 5mm (1/4in) wide and only require soaking in boiling water for about 10 minutes. They are simple and easy to prepare and are found in supermarkets and Asian food stores.
**Rice vermicelli noodles** These are made from rice and water, like all the rice noodles, and are probably the most widely used noodles in Vietnam. They are readily available in most supermarkets. Soak in hot water and use in salads and stir-fries or deep-fry. When deep-fried they puff and become crispy.
**Somen noodles** These are wheat-based noodles that are mainly used in the Japanese cuisine and are widely used by the Vietnamese. They are long thin white noodles wrapped in bundles.
**Wheat noodles** Sold fresh, these noodles are thick and are made from wheat and water.

## Oil

Use a light flavoured oil in these recipes such as safflower oil or even extra light olive oil which has virtually no flavour. Canola oil could also be used.

## Oyster Sauce

This sauce contains oyster extract and is a rich dark brown colour. It adds a rich flavour and is used sparingly as it is quite salty. There is no substitute for this sauce.

## Palm Sugar (gula jawa)

Is made from the sap of the coconut palm tree and has an almost caramel flavour. You will usually find it in cylinders or blocks. I find it easier to grate the sugar as it is very hard and compact unlike white sugar. You can use brown sugar, but the dish will not have quite the same flavour.

## Pickled Mustard

Made from the green mustard cabbage, pickled mustard is the young and tender heart of the plant preserved or pickled in brine. It is sold at most Asian food stores in vacuum sealed packets.

## Rice

Jasmine rice, glutinous rice and long-grain rice are most commonly used and are found in supermarkets and Asian food stores.

## Rice Paper

Used for making fresh spring rolls. You can find it in Asian food stores. Soak the rice paper in warm water until just soft before using.

## Rice Vinegar

Not as sour as regular vinegars, rice vinegar has a delicate sweetness and is milder than white vinegar.

## Sambal Oelek

Sambal oelek is a chilli paste made from red chillies, vinegar and salt. It is not a traditional ingredient but is used often throughout the book simply because it adds a delicious flavour and colour. It is found in supermarkets and Asian food stores.

## Sesame Oil

Made from toasted sesame seeds. It has a smoky flavour and is added to stir-fries and other dishes in small quantities – a little goes a long way. It is not usually used for frying.

## Shrimp Paste

This paste is very strong smelling but adds a delicious flavour to many dishes. Shrimp paste must be cooked first then used in the recipe. Don't let the odour put you off, as shrimp paste is quite subtle in the finished recipe.

## Soy Sauce

Use a light soy sauce from Asian food stores or supermarkets. It is made from fermented soy beans.

## Split Yellow Mung Beans

These are the dried yellow beans that have been split and are sold in packets in most Asian food stores. They do not require soaking.

## Spring Roll Wrappers

These can be found in supermarkets and Asian food stores and come in several sizes. Use the size mentioned in the recipes. There is not a substitute.

## Sugar Cane

Fresh sugar cane can be found in Asian, Indian and Caribbean food stores, but is more readily available in cans. Fresh sugar cane needs to be peeled first, but the canned sugar cane is ready to use immediately.

## Sweet Chilli Sauce

A spicy but sweet sauce that goes with all types of Thai food from appetisers to noodles. It is found in supermarkets and Asian food stores. A must to have.

## Tamarind

Tamarind has a tart flavour. It is available as a purée or concentrate. Use half the amount of concentrate to purée. Use vinegar or lemon juice as a substitute.

## Taro

Taro root is an oval shaped tuber that has a brown hairy skin. It is creamy and smooth like a potato and it can be substituted with white sweet potato.

## Tofu, Firm or Hard (bean curd)

The best tofu or bean curd to buy is from Asian food stores or health food stores. The firmer the tofu, the better it is to stir-fry or pan-fry. Tofu is an excellent source of protein made from soy beans. It marinates well, soaking in all the flavours around it. Keep leftover tofu in a deep dish covered with water for up to a few days, changing the water daily.

## Wonton Wrappers

Available in rounds or squares roughly 8cm (3in) wide. You will find them in Asian food stores in the refrigerator. You can use gow gees pastry rounds or squares instead.

# Appetisers and Snacks

I n Thailand, entrees or appetisers are not usually eaten
before a main meal. Instead, appetisers and snacks are
eaten during the day and these are purchased from the
many street food vendors selling tasty morsels. A large
variety of foods from Vietnam, Laos and Cambodia are
suitable for serving as appetisers as many dishes are made
in small packages or in small portions.

The appetisers and snacks in the following pages can be
served at cocktail parties, as an entree to an Asian meal or
for most entertaining situations. Delicious dipping sauces
are often served with them and add an extra dimension to
the exotic flavours.

*RIGHT: Witlof with Chilli Pork*

# Witlof with Chilli Pork

This can be a stylish appetiser for entertaining or, for a more casual appearance, serve with vegetable squares such as capsicums (peppers) or fill small fresh mushrooms with the mixture. The Chilli Pork can be made several hours ahead and warmed before serving.

*1 tablespoon oil*
*2 cloves garlic, crushed*
*1 tablespoon finely chopped fresh ginger*
*4 green shallots (spring onions), finely chopped*
*$1/2$ teaspoon shrimp paste*
*1 tablespoon chopped lemon grass*
*2 teaspoons sambal oelek*
*150g (5oz) pork fillet, finely chopped*
*250g (8oz) cherry tomatoes, quartered*
*1 tablespoon coconut cream*
*3 tablespoons chopped fresh coriander*
*1 witlof (Belgian endive)*

Heat the oil in a frying pan and add the garlic, ginger, green shallots (spring onions), shrimp paste, lemon grass and sambal oelek. Cook the mixture stirring until the green shallots are soft.

Add the pork and cook stirring until the pork just begins to turn white. Stir in the tomatoes and the coconut cream then bring to a boil. Simmer the mixture uncovered until it thickens and the tomatoes are well cooked. Stir in the coriander.

While the mixture is simmering, carefully separate the witlof (Belgian endive) leaves, wash and drain well. Spoon the chilli pork mixture onto the witlof just before serving.

SERVES 4

# Sesame Prawn Toasts

This appetiser is simple to prepare and can be made several hours ahead. Assemble and grill the toasts just before serving. They go wonderfully with pre-dinner drinks or served at that afternoon get together.

*4 slices thick-sliced bread*
*1 tablespoon oil*
*60g (2oz) minced pork*
*8 uncooked large prawns, peeled, deveined and chopped*
*1 large clove garlic, crushed*
*1 egg white*
*2 tablespoons sesame seeds*
*2 tablespoons chopped fresh coriander*
*$1/4$ teaspoon chilli powder*
*ground black pepper*

Cut the bread into 5cm (2in) rounds using a cutter. You should be able to cut 3 rounds from each slice. Toast the rounds lightly on both sides under a hot grill.

Heat the oil in a frying pan, add the pork and cook stirring until just cooked. Add the prawns and garlic and stir until just cooked; cool. Combine the pork mixture with the egg white, seeds, coriander, chilli powder and the pepper in a bowl.

Spoon the pork mixture onto the toast rounds, pressing lightly and forming a mound on each one. Place the toasts on a baking tray and cook under a hot grill until heated through and crispy and browned on top.

MAKES ABOUT 12

~ 16 ~

# Pork and Crab Cubes

The cubes can be made a day ahead and served cold or cooked an hour or so ahead and then served warm.

*170g (5¹/₂oz) can crab meat, drained and flaked*
*1 single chicken breast fillet, very finely chopped*
*150g (5oz) lean minced pork*
*4 green shallots (spring onions), finely chopped*
*2 tablespoons chopped fresh coriander*
*1 egg, lightly beaten*
*1 tablespoon coconut cream*
*1 tablespoon Thai sweet chilli sauce*
*extra coriander leaves*

Combine all the ingredients except the extra coriander leaves in a bowl and mix well. Spoon into a foil lined 8cm x 26cm (3in x 10in) cake pan, pressing firmly. Cover the pan tightly with foil.

Place the pan in a bamboo steamer over a wok one-quarter filled with boiling water. Cover the steamer and cook over gently boiling water for 30 minutes.

Remove from the steamer, remove the foil and drain away any excess liquid in the pan. Stand the loaf for 40 minutes.

Turn the loaf onto a board and cut into 4cm (1¹/₂in) cubes, top each cube with an extra coriander leaf then a toothpick (cocktail stick) before serving.

MAKES ABOUT 12

## ~ Tip ~

You can also steam food in a double boiler or a saucepan steamer. If you don't have either, place the food on a rack over a baking dish half filled with boiling water. Cover the whole thing with foil and bake in a 180°C (350°F) oven for the required time. Check the food is cooked before turning off the oven as it may take a little longer.

# Pan-Fried Fish Cakes

This is a very simple method of making delicious Thai-flavoured fish cakes which can be made in the size I suggest, or you could make them even smaller to serve at cocktail parties.

*400g (12¹/₂oz) boneless fish fillets*
*2 teaspoons good quality purchased or home-made red curry paste*
*1 egg*
*4 green shallots (spring onions), chopped*
*1 teaspoon grated lime zest*
*2 tablespoons chopped fresh coriander*
*1 tablespoon oil*

Process the fish, curry paste and egg until finely chopped. Add the green shallots (spring onions), lime zest and coriander. Wet your hands slightly then shape 2 tablespoons of the mixture into a patty. Repeat with the remaining mixture.

Heat the oil in a non-stick frying pan, add the fish cakes and cook until lightly browned underneath then turn and cook the other side until cooked through. Serve them with Chilli and Peanut Sauce (see THE ESSENTIALS).

MAKES ABOUT 10

# Steamed Spicy Vegetarian Buns

1 x 7g (¼oz) sachet dry yeast
½ cup (125ml/4fl oz) warm water
¼ cup (60g/2oz) caster sugar
1 cup (150g/5oz) plain flour
½ cup (75g/2½oz) self-raising flour
15g (½oz) butter, melted
FILLING
1 Chinese dried mushroom
50g (1½oz) firm tofu
2 teaspoons sesame oil
½ small leek, finely chopped
2 cloves garlic, crushed
1 teaspoon grated fresh ginger
1 tablespoon lime juice
½ small carrot, grated
1 tablespoon roasted unsalted cashew nuts
2 teaspoons sweet chilli sauce
1 tablespoon chopped fresh mint
2 teaspoons bean sauce
3 teaspoons tomato paste

Combine the yeast, 2 tablespoons of the warm water, 1 teaspoon of the sugar and 1 teaspoon of the plain flour in a small bowl. Cover, stand in a warm place for about 15 minutes or until frothy. Sift the remaining flours into a large bowl, add the remaining sugar, mix well. Stir in the yeast mixture, remaining water and butter, mix to a soft dough. Knead on a floured surface about 3 minutes or until smooth and elastic. Place in a lightly oiled bowl, cover with greased plastic wrap, stand in a warm place about 1 hour or until doubled.

Make the filling at this stage. Cover the mushroom with hot water in a bowl, stand for 30 minutes, drain. Finely chop the mushroom, discarding the stem. Cut the tofu into 5mm (¼in) cubes. Heat the sesame oil in a frying pan, add the leek, garlic and ginger, and cook for about 3 minutes or until soft, cool. Stir in the mushroom, tofu, lime juice, carrot, chopped cashew nuts, chilli sauce, mint, bean sauce and tomato paste.

Knead the dough on a floured surface for about 5 minutes or until smooth, divide into 16 portions. Roll each portion into a ball, flatten into a large round. Spoon 2 level teaspoons of filling onto the centre of each round, gather the edges to enclose the filling then pinch the tops to seal and form a round bun.

Lightly brush 16 x 9cm (3½in) squares of greaseproof paper with sesame oil, top with the buns, pinched-side up, then place in a large bamboo steamer. Steam for about 8 minutes or until the buns are dry to touch. If your steamer is small, steam in 2 batches.

MAKES 16 BUNS

# Prawns with Leeks in Fish Sauce

8 medium uncooked prawns
¼ teaspoon freshly ground black pepper
3 cloves garlic, crushed
2 tablespoons oil
1 leek, sliced
1½ tablespoons fish sauce
2 tablespoons lime juice
1 tablespoon chopped fresh garlic chives

Peel and devein the prawns, leaving the tails intact. Combine the prawns with the pepper and half the crushed garlic.

Heat half the oil in a wok or frying pan, add the leek and remaining garlic, stir-fry for 2 minutes or until the leek is just soft. Place the leek onto serving plates, keep warm while preparing the prawns.

Heat the remaining oil in the same wok, add the prawn mixture, stir-fry over high heat for about 3 minutes or until the prawns are just cooked. Stir in the fish sauce and lime juice. Serve the prawns on leeks, drizzled with pan juices and sprinkled with chives.

SERVES 2

*LEFT: From top: Steamed Spicy Vegetarian Buns; Prawns with Leeks in Fish Sauce*

# Chicken and Coriander Rounds

Make the rounds a day ahead for time saving on the day.

*2 tablespoons oil*
*2 teaspoons good quality purchased or home-made*
*green curry paste*
*1 clove garlic, crushed*
*1 small onion, chopped*
*1/2 small red capsicum (pepper), finely chopped*
*300g (9 1/2oz) chicken thigh fillets, chopped*
*1 egg, lightly beaten*
FILLING
*1 cup (30g/1oz) fresh coriander leaves*
*1/2 cup (15g/1/2oz) chopped garlic chives*
*1 teaspoon good quality purchased or home-made*
*green curry paste*

Heat the oil in a frying pan, add the curry paste, garlic, onion and capsicum (pepper), cook over low heat about 5 minutes or until the onion is very soft; cool.

Process the chicken with the onion mixture and the egg to a paste consistency, remove from the processor.

Make the filling by processing all the filling ingredients with 2 tablespoons of the processed chicken mixture until well chopped.

Divide the chicken mixture into 6 even portions. Spread 1 portion on a 25cm (10in) square of baking paper into a 12cm (4 1/2in) square. Spoon one-third of the filling mixture along the centre of the chicken mixture.

Spoon another portion of chicken mixture over the top of the filling and spread to cover the filling. Roll up firmly in the baking paper, shaping into a sausage, and twist the ends of the paper to seal. Repeat with the remaining chicken mixture and filling. Place the rolls into a bamboo steamer and place in a wok one-quarter filled with boiling water. Steam the rolls over gently boiling water for 20 minutes.

Remove the rolls from the wok, loosen the paper and drain away any liquid. Stand for 15 minutes before cutting diagonally into 1cm (1/2in) thick slices.

MAKES ABOUT 30

Spreading the chicken mixture over the filling.

Roll up firmly and twist the ends of the paper to seal.

*RIGHT: Chicken and Coriander Rounds*

# Garlic Herb Oysters

This aromatic mix of herbs makes the oysters taste delicious, especially when cooked in the butter, but they must be eaten warm. However, if you are planning to serve them cold, cook the oysters in 2 teaspoons of oil instead of the butter.

*12 fresh oysters in half shells*
*3 teaspoons butter*
*2 teaspoons fish sauce*
*1 clove garlic, crushed*
*1 small red chilli, seeded and finely chopped*
*1 teaspoon grated fresh ginger*
*1 teaspoon finely chopped lemon grass*
*1 teaspoon chopped fresh mint*
*2 teaspoons lime juice*

Remove the oysters from their shells and reserve shells. Heat the butter and the fish sauce in a small frying pan, add the garlic, chilli, ginger and lemon grass and stir over heat for about 1 minute or until the mixture begins to foam, then add the oysters, toss until well coated and heated through.

Place the oysters back in their shells, sprinkle with mint and drizzle with the lime juice.

SERVES 2

# Beef Omelette Scrolls

These attractive little appetisers are best eaten warm. They can be made up to 4 hours ahead and reheated.

*2 eggs*
*2 tablespoons plain flour*
*2 teaspoons chopped fresh garlic chives*
*1 tablespoon milk*
*2 teaspoons fish sauce*
*1 tablespoon oil*
*1½ tablespoons coconut cream*
*1 teaspoon fish sauce, extra*
*8 fresh mint leaves*
BEEF FILLING
*350g (11oz) beef fillet or rump steak*
*3 teaspoons fish sauce*
*2 cloves garlic, crushed*
*2 tablespoons lemon juice*
*1 teaspoon sesame oil*
*2 teaspoons oil*
*1 teaspoon grated lemon zest*
*2 tablespoons roasted unsalted cashew nuts, finely chopped*

Beat the eggs, flour, garlic chives, milk and fish sauce in bowl until smooth. Heat half the oil in a 23cm (9in) omelette pan, pour in half the egg mixture, swirl the pan so the mixture covers the base. Cook gently until set. Slide the omelette onto a board then cut into quarters. Repeat with the remaining mixture.

Make the beef filling by cutting the beef into strips 3mm (⅛in) thick. Combine the beef, fish sauce, garlic and lemon juice in medium bowl. Cover and refrigerate for at least 1 hour or overnight.

Heat the oils in a medium frying pan, add the beef mixture, stir-fry until the beef is just cooked. Transfer to a bowl, add the zest and cashew nuts, mix well.

Spread each omelette quarter with some combined coconut cream and extra fish sauce. Place some beef strips along the centre, top with a mint leaf, fold over the corners then secure with toothpicks and serve.

MAKES 8

# Fresh Chicken and Crab Spring Rolls

These spring rolls cannot be made too far ahead because the rice paper dries out too quickly. Most of your time is spent on the preparation of the fillings, so have the fillings and Fish Dipping Sauce all prepared ahead and then make the spring rolls close to serving.

1 teaspoon honey
$^1/_4$ teaspoon chilli powder
1 tablespoon rice vinegar
1 single chicken breast fillet
2 teaspoons fish sauce
60g (2oz) rice vermicelli noodles
3 Chinese dried mushrooms
$^1/_2$ cup (40g/about $1^1/_2$oz) bean sprouts
1 small carrot, grated
3 green shallots (spring onions), chopped
2 pickled cucumbers or gherkins, finely sliced
2 lettuce leaves (butter or iceberg lettuce), finely shredded
75g ($2^1/_2$oz) cooked crab meat
$^1/_4$ cup (7g/$^1/_4$oz) fresh sprigs of coriander
$^1/_2$ cup (15g/$^1/_2$oz) fresh mint leaves
12 x 16cm ($6^1/_2$in) rounds of rice paper
2 teaspoons roasted unsalted peanuts, finely chopped

Combine the honey, chilli powder and vinegar in a bowl, add the chicken and stir until the chicken is well coated. Cover, and refrigerate for at least 1 hour or overnight. Cook the chicken under a hot grill until cooked through, cool. Slice the chicken thinly then drizzle with the fish sauce.

Place the vermicelli in a heatproof bowl, cover with boiling water, stand for 30 minutes, drain. Using scissors, cut the vermicelli into shorter lengths.

Place the mushrooms in a bowl, cover with hot water, stand for 30 minutes, drain. Slice the mushrooms thinly, discarding the tough stems.

Set up the fillings on a bench in order of use for rolling the spring rolls. First the chicken, then vermicelli, mushrooms, beans sprouts, carrot, green shallots (spring onions), cucumber, lettuce, crab meat, coriander and mint. Have a bowl of warm water nearby large enough for the rice paper.

Soak a sheet of rice paper in the water for about 20 seconds or until just pliable then place on a board. Place some chicken, vermicelli, mushrooms, sprouts, carrot, green shallots, cucumber, lettuce, crab meat, coriander and mint on the base end of the rice paper, roll up firmly but carefully, folding in the sides. Work quickly to avoid the rice paper from drying out. Repeat with the remaining rice paper and fillings. Place on a serving plate and serve immediately or cover with plastic wrap and refrigerate for up to 3 hours.

Serve the rolls with the Fish Dipping Sauce (see THE ESSENTIALS) sprinkled with peanuts.

MAKES 12

~ Tip ~

To make your own chilli powder, grind dried chillies in a coffee grinder, blender or mortar and pestle until a powder. Store in a clean jar.

# Skewered Saté Prawns

The prawns can be prepared a day ahead and then quickly grilled or barbecued just before serving. This is a very popular appetiser and it's not too spicy.

*12 uncooked king prawns*
*1 clove garlic, crushed*
*1 tablespoon peanut butter*
*2 tablespoons very finely chopped onion*
*2 teaspoons Thai fish sauce*
*1/2 cup (125ml/4fl oz) coconut cream*
*1/4 teaspoon chilli powder (more if preferred)*
*1/2 teaspoon ground turmeric*

Peel the prawns and leave the tails intact. Place the prawns on the ends of short bamboo skewers, skewering through the end and just above the tail of each prawn. Place the prawns in a dish or jug keeping the skewer ends out of the base.

Combine all the remaining ingredients in a bowl and pour over the prawns in the dish making sure all the prawns are well coated. Cover the prawns and refrigerate for at least several hours or overnight to allow the flavours to develop.

Grill or barbecue the prawn satés, turning during cooking, and brushing with any remaining marinade in the dish, until just cooked through. Serve immediately.

SERVES 3 TO 4

# Lime and Pork Patties

Make this mixture a day ahead, shape into patties and cook close to serving. The lime flavour gives the patties a zesty tang.

*250g (8oz) lean minced pork*
*2 cloves garlic, crushed*
*1 teaspoon grated lime zest*
*1 tablespoon Thai fish sauce*
*2 teaspoons oyster sauce*
*2 teaspoons sambal oelek*
*1/4 cup (15g/1/2oz) finely chopped green shallots (spring onions)*
*1 egg white*
*1 tablespoon oil*

Combine all the ingredients in a bowl and mix well. Shape tablespoons of the mixture into little patties.

Heat the oil in a frying pan, add the patties in a single layer and cook until lightly browned underneath. Turn the patties and cook on the other side until browned and just cooked through. Don't overcook the patties or they will become dry.

Serve the patties with Chilli Lime Sauce (see THE ESSENTIALS).

MAKES ABOUT 15

*LEFT: From top: Skewered Saté Prawns; Lime and Pork Patties*

# Chicken and Corn Wedges

Baking this recipe makes it a healthy alternative to frying and there is no last minute cooking to do – you can pop them in the oven while preparing other dishes.

*3 eggs*
*270g (9oz) can corn kernels*
*2¹/₂ tablespoons plain flour, sifted*
*1 cup ((200g/6¹/₂oz) finely chopped cooked chicken*
*¹/₂ teaspoon grated lime zest*
*1 medium red chilli, finely chopped*
*1 tablespoon chopped fresh mint*
*1 tablespoon chopped fresh coriander*
*2 teaspoons Thai fish sauce*

Combine all the ingredients in a bowl and mix well. Spoon the mixture into a greased and lined 18cm (7in) round cake pan. Bake in a 160°C (325°F) oven for about 20 minutes or until cooked in the centre.

Cool for 10 minutes then turn onto a board and cut into wedges. You can serve the wedges with bottled Thai sweet chilli sauce.

MAKES ABOUT 12 WEDGES

# Crisp Cashew Bags

This is a simpler version of the deep-fried pouches often seen in Thai restaurants. The baking eliminates messy deep-frying and extra oil.

*1 clove garlic, crushed*
*¹/₂ cup (80g/2¹/₂oz) raw cashew nuts*
*¹/₂ cup (80g/2¹/₂oz) finely grated carrot*
*2 tablespoons sesame seeds, toasted*
*¹/₄ cup (7g/¹/₄oz) finely chopped garlic chives*
*1 teaspoon Thai fish sauce*
*1 tablespoon chopped fresh coriander*
*1 tablespoon oil*
*20 x 8cm (3in) square egg pastry sheets*
*1 teaspoon cornflour*
*1 tablespoon water*
*1 tablespoon oil, extra*

Process the garlic, cashew nuts, carrot, sesame seeds, garlic chives, fish sauce, coriander and oil until finely chopped.

Spoon 2 teaspoons of the mixture onto a pastry sheet, brush the edges with the combined cornflour and water. Gather the edges of the pastry sheet around the filling and pinch firmly to form a little bag.

Brush the bag lightly with the extra oil and place onto a lightly greased baking tray. Repeat with the remaining filling, pastry sheets, cornflour mixture and oil. Bake the bags in a 200°C (400°F) oven for about 10 minutes or until lightly browned all over. You can serve them with bottled Thai sweet chilli sauce.

MAKES 20

~ Tip ~

To toast sesame seeds, place them in a pan and stir constantly over medium heat until lightly browned. Remove the seeds from the pan to cool.

# Oven-Baked Spring Rolls

*50g (1¹/₂oz) bean thread vermicelli noodles*
*1 tablespoon oil*
*125g (4oz) lean minced pork*
*8 uncooked large prawns, peeled, deveined and*
*finely chopped*
*1 large clove garlic, chopped*
*2 coriander roots, finely chopped*
*4 green shallots (spring onions), finely chopped*
*2.5cm (1in) piece fresh ginger, finely shredded*
*1 teaspoon sambal oelek*
*2 tablespoons chopped fresh coriander leaves*
*26 spring roll wrappers*
*3 teaspoons cornflour*
*1 tablespoon water*
*oil, extra*

Place the noodles in a heatproof bowl, cover with hot water, soak for 10 minutes. Drain the noodles and cut into 5cm (2in) lengths.

Heat the oil in a frying pan, add the pork, prawns, garlic, coriander roots, green shallots (spring onions), ginger and sambal oelek. Cook, stirring until the prawns are just cooked; cool. Stir in the noodles and chopped coriander and mix well.

Place a tablespoon of noodle mixture onto a spring roll wrapper, brush the edges with the combined cornflour and water. Fold in the sides and roll up firmly. Place seam side down on an oiled baking tray, brush lightly with oil.

Repeat with the remaining noodle mixture, spring roll wrappers, cornflour mixture and oil. Bake the rolls in a 200°C (400°F) oven for about 20 minutes or until lightly browned and crisp.

You can serve the rolls with bottled Thai sweet chilli sauce or Chilli and Peanut Sauce (see THE ESSENTIALS).

MAKES 26

# Lemon Grass Mussels

You can prepare these mussels several hours ahead and cook them just before serving. Smaller mussels are delicious in this recipe and are a nice size for appetisers.

*20 small black mussels*
*1 single chicken breast fillet, chopped*
*2 teaspoons good quality purchased or home-made*
*green curry paste*
*¹/₂ small onion, finely chopped*
*¹/₂ small carrot, finely grated*
*1¹/₂ tablespoons chopped lemon grass*

Scrub and debeard the mussels by pulling away the fibrous bits protruding from between the shell halves.

Place the mussels in a large pan with a little water. Cover and bring to a boil. Remove the lid and remove the mussels from the pan as they open; cool. Remove one half shell from each mussel and discard. Loosen the mussel meat in the remaining half shells.

Process all the remaining ingredients together until finely chopped. Spoon the chicken mixture onto the mussels, shaping around the mussel meat.

Grill the mussels until lightly browned and the topping is cooked through. You can serve the mussels topped with a squeeze of lemon juice and chopped fresh coriander.

MAKES 20

# Barbecued Prawns on Sugar Cane

These unusual appetisers are one of the delights of Vietnamese cuisine. When the sugar cane sticks are barbecued, the ends will char and have a delicious raw sweetness once you eat through the prawn mixture and start chewing on the sugar cane. If you cannot find sugar cane, use stalks of fresh lemon grass instead.

*600g (19oz) medium uncooked prawns*
*4 cloves garlic, crushed*
*4 green shallots (spring onions), chopped*
*2 teaspoons caster sugar*
*2 teaspoons fish sauce*
*2 teaspoons cornflour*
*1 bacon rasher, finely chopped*
*5 x 14cm (5¹/₂in) long sticks canned sugar cane*
*2 teaspoons roasted unsalted peanuts, chopped*

Peel and devein the prawns. Process the prawns, garlic, green shallots (spring onions), sugar, fish sauce, cornflour and bacon until fine and pasty. Cut the sugar cane sticks in half. With lightly oiled hands, mould level tablespoons of prawn mixture around the centre of the sugar cane sticks.

Heat a greased barbecue hotplate, griddle pan or grill until hot, barbecue or grill the sticks until the prawn mixture is cooked through, turning occasionally during cooking.

Serve with a small bowl of Fish Dipping Sauce (see THE ESSENTIALS) sprinkled with chopped peanuts for each person.

MAKES ABOUT 10

Process the prawn mixture until fine and pasty.

Mould level tablespoons of the prawn mixture around the sugar cane sticks.

*RIGHT: Barbecued Prawns on Sugar Cane*

## Sesame Lamb and Baby Onion Sticks

Lamb backstrap is a larger piece of the lamb fillet, but you can use lamb fillets or beef fillet instead.

*350g (11oz) lamb backstrap*
*1 clove garlic, crushed*
*1 teaspoon grated fresh ginger*
*1 tablespoon lime juice*
*¼ teaspoon paprika*
*2 teaspoons chopped fresh coriander*
*1½ tablespoons fish sauce*
*4 small brown pickling onions, halved*
*1 quantity Peanut Sauce (see THE ESSENTIALS)*
*2 teaspoons sesame seeds, toasted*
*2 teaspoons sesame oil*
*1 tablespoon sesame seeds, toasted, extra*
*2 teaspoons chopped fresh coriander*

Cut the lamb into 3cm (1¼in) pieces. Combine the lamb, garlic, ginger, lime juice, paprika, coriander, fish sauce and onions in a bowl. Cover and refrigerate for at least 1 hour or overnight, stirring occasionally.

Drain the lamb and the onions from the marinade, reserve the marinade. Divide the lamb and onion pieces into 8 portions and thread onto bamboo skewers. Grill or barbecue until the lamb is just cooked, turning once during cooking.

While the lamb sticks are cooking, prepare the dipping sauce by combining the Peanut Sauce with the sesame seeds and sesame oil in a small bowl. Serve the sticks sprinkled with the extra sesame seeds and coriander and accompanied by the dipping sauce.

MAKES 8

### ~ Tip ~
To avoid burning the bamboo skewers during cooking, soak them in water for about 1 hour before using them.

## Oven-Baked Marinated Pork Fillet

A healthier alternative to pork spare ribs, the pork fillet is free of fat and is very tender. This baked pork fillet can be used instead of bought barbecued pork in any recipe. Eat it hot or cold, served in thin slices as an appetiser with some Fish Dipping Sauce (see THE ESSENTIALS). If you prefer to use pork spare ribs, you will need about 600g (19oz) of spare ribs.

*2 tablespoons caster sugar*
*1 tablespoon fish sauce*
*2 cloves garlic, crushed*
*1 tablespoon chopped lemon grass*
*½ teaspoon five spice powder*
*½ teaspoon dried chilli flakes*
*2 teaspoons rice vinegar*
*1 tablespoon chopped fresh mint*
*1 tablespoon tomato paste*
*1 clove garlic, extra*
*300g (9½oz) pork fillet*

Using a mortar and pestle or a blender, blend the sugar, fish sauce, garlic, lemon grass, five spice powder, chilli flakes, vinegar, mint and tomato paste until smooth.

Cut the extra garlic clove into 6 thin strips. Make 6 small incisions in the pork fillet, and insert the garlic strips. Brush the marinade mixture all over the pork, cover, and refrigerate for at least 2 hours or overnight to allow the flavours to develop.

Place the pork on a wire rack over a baking tray, add a little water to the tray to prevent any juices from burning. Bake the pork in a 200°C (400°F) oven for about 40 minutes or until just cooked through. Cool slightly before slicing.

SERVES 4 TO 6

# Curried Pork Turnovers

Taro is becoming more available when in season but if you cannot find any, substitute white sweet potato which will give the dough a lovely delicate sweetness.

250g (8oz) taro, peeled and chopped
30g (1oz) butter, chopped
1/4 cup (40g/about 1 1/2oz) plain flour
3 teaspoons black sesame seeds or toasted white sesame seeds
Shallot Oil (see THE ESSENTIALS)
FILLING
125g (4oz) pork mince
2 teaspoons finely chopped garlic chives
1 teaspoon fish sauce
2 teaspoons oil
1 tablespoon finely chopped lemon grass
1 small onion, finely chopped
2 teaspoons curry powder
2 teaspoons chopped fresh coriander

Boil or steam the taro until tender, mash with the butter until completely smooth, cool. Combine the mashed taro with the flour and sesame seeds in a bowl.

Make the filling by combining the pork mince, garlic chives and fish sauce in a bowl. Cover and refrigerate for 1 hour. Heat the oil in a wok or frying pan, add the lemon grass, onion, curry powder and coriander, cook for 1 minute or until aromatic. Add the pork mixture, cook over high heat, breaking up lumps, until the mixture is dry and changed colour. Cool.

Divide the taro dough into 12 portions, flatten each portion into an 8cm (3in) round on a lightly floured surface, using the floured palm of your hand.

Spoon 2 level teaspoons of the filling onto the centre of each round of dough, fold over to enclose the filling, pinch the edges to seal or press with a fork.

Place turnovers onto a lightly greased baking tray, brush with Shallot Oil, bake in a 200°C (400°F) oven for 10 minutes, turn the turnovers, brush with more oil, bake a further 8 minutes or until well browned.

MAKES 12

# Tomato Dip with Vegetable Crudités

This dip is ideal for people on a weight-reduction diet. It contains no added fat and is a wonderful blend of flavours cooked down to a spicy dip. It can be made up to 3 days ahead. Use any vegetables for crudités.

5 small ripe tomatoes
3 cloves garlic
2 small red onions, finely chopped
2 teaspoons chopped fresh coriander root
1 long green chilli, finely chopped
1 teaspoon tomato paste
1 teaspoon fish sauce
3 teaspoons chopped fresh coriander
50g (about 1 1/2oz) okra
100g (3 1/2oz) cauliflower or broccoli, cut into small florets
25g (about 1oz) snow peas (mangetout)
1 small red or green capsicum (pepper), cut into thick strips

Skin the tomatoes by making a large cross in the base end of each tomato, just cutting through the skin. Add the tomatoes to a pan of boiling water, bring water back to the boil, boil for 1 minute, drain, rinse under cold water. Peel away the skin from the base end.

Bruise the garlic by flattening it with the flat side of a knife, then coarsely chop it. Add the garlic, onions, coriander and chilli to a wok or medium saucepan. Cook over heat, stirring constantly to avoid burning, for 1 minute or until aromatic. Add the tomatoes, stir over heat until well combined. Allow the mixture to simmer, uncovered for about 8 minutes or until thick, stirring occasionally. Add the tomato paste and fish sauce, mix well.

Spoon the dip into a serving bowl, sprinkle with the coriander and serve with vegetable crudités.

MAKES ABOUT 3/4 CUP

# Chicken and Rice Noodle Soup

This soup is traditionally made with beef and quite often is served for breakfast. I make it with chicken and find it makes a great lunch or light dinner.

*1 single chicken breast fillet*
*2.5cm (1in) piece fresh ginger*
*3 cups (750ml/24fl oz) well-flavoured chicken stock*
*1 star anise*
*2.5cm (1in) cinnamon stick*
*1 small onion, chopped*
*3 teaspoons fish sauce*
*250g (8oz) fresh rice noodles (banh pho)*
*2 small red chillies, finely sliced*
*2 green shallots (spring onions), finely sliced*
*1 tablespoon fresh coriander leaves*
*1 tablespoon small fresh mint leaves*

Cut the chicken into 3mm (1/8in) slices. Peel the ginger and cut into very fine sticks. Combine the stock with half the ginger, star anise, cinnamon, onion and fish sauce in a saucepan, bring to the boil then reduce the heat and simmer, covered, for 10 minutes. Strain the stock into a jug and discard the onion mixture.

Return the stock to the pan, bring to a simmer and add the chicken. Simmer for about 5 minutes or until the chicken is just cooked. Meanwhile, place the noodles in a heatproof bowl, cover with boiling water and stand while the chicken is cooking. Drain the noodles, place into soup bowls and top with the chicken mixture. Serve the soup sprinkled with the chillies, green shallots (spring onions), coriander and mint. Have some lime wedges and a mild chilli sauce on the table for flavouring the soup.

SERVES 2

VARIATION
This soup can be made with beef stock and thinly sliced beef fillet for a traditional flavour

# Lemon and Dill Seafood Soup

Use lemon leaves that are chemical free, or if unavailable, double the lemon grass. Be sure to fold the leaves along the centre vein to release their aroma during cooking.

*1 Chinese dried mushroom*
*200g (6$\frac{1}{2}$oz) ling fillets*
*4 large uncooked prawns, peeled and deveined*
*2 teaspoons fish sauce*
*$\frac{1}{2}$ teaspoon freshly ground black pepper*
*2 cloves garlic, sliced*
*3 green shallots (spring onions), sliced*
*2 fresh lemon leaves*
*1 tablespoon chopped fresh lemon grass*
*1 tablespoon tamarind purée*
*3 cups (750ml/24fl oz) well-flavoured fish stock or water*
*1 small tomato, peeled, seeded and finely chopped*
*1 tablespoon chopped fresh dill*
*1 small red chilli, finely chopped*
*$\frac{1}{2}$ cup (40g/about 1$\frac{1}{2}$oz) bean sprouts*

Soak the mushroom in hot water for 30 minutes, drain. Remove the stem and cut the mushroom into quarters. Cut the ling into 2.5cm (1in) pieces. Combine the ling, prawns, fish sauce and pepper in a bowl, cover, refrigerate 30 minutes.

Combine the garlic, green shallots (spring onions), lemon leaves, lemon grass and tamarind in a wok or frying pan. Stir over heat about 1 minute or until aromatic. Add the stock and tomato, bring to the boil, add the mushroom and fish mixture, simmer uncovered for about 2 minutes or until the seafood is tender. Discard lemon leaves. Stir in the dill and chilli.

Place some bean sprouts into each soup bowl, ladle hot soup over the sprouts and serve immediately.

SERVES 4 AS AN ENTREE OR
2 AS A MAIN COURSE

# Tomato and Egg Thread Soup

The tamarind purée gives this vegetarian soup its tangy flavour. You can use any vegetables available such as broccoli or green beans, instead of the pumpkin, cauliflower and snow peas (mangetout).

*100g (3½oz) pumpkin or swede*
*75g (2½oz) cauliflower*
*50g (about 1½oz) snow peas (mangetout)*
*2 teaspoons oil*
*2 teaspoons chopped fresh coriander root*
*1½ teaspoons galangal powder*
*2 teaspoons fish sauce*
*1 ripe tomato, peeled and chopped*
*1 cup (250ml/8fl oz) well-flavoured vegetable stock*
*1 cup (250ml/8fl oz) water*
*2 teaspoons tamarind purée*
*2 teaspoons lime juice*
*2 green shallots (spring onions), sliced diagonally*
*2 tablespoons chopped fresh coriander*
*1 egg, lightly beaten*
*1 tablespoon fresh coriander leaves*

Cut the pumpkin into 2cm (¾in) cubes. Cut the cauliflower into small florets. Cut the snow peas (mangetout) diagonally into 1cm (½in) wide strips.

Heat the oil in a wok or frying pan, add the coriander root, galangal, fish sauce, and tomato, stir-fry about 1 minute or until aromatic. Add the stock, water and tamarind purée, bring to the boil. Add the pumpkin and cauliflower, simmer uncovered for 4 minutes. Add the snow peas, lime juice, green shallots (spring onions) and coriander, bring to the boil. While boiling, pour in the beaten egg in a thin stream, stirring continuously to form threads. Garnish with extra coriander leaves and serve.

SERVES 2

# Aromatic Beef and Aniseed Soup

Ideal for a cold winter's dinner, this soup is best made a day ahead to allow the flavours from the spices to develop. Make the soup without adding the vegetables, then just before serving, bring the soup to a boil, and add the zucchini, carrot, bean sauce and lime juice.

*300g (9½oz) beef blade steak*
*½ small zucchini (courgette)*
*½ small carrot*
*1 tablespoon oil*
*1 clove garlic, crushed*
*1 onion, finely chopped*
*2 medium ripe tomatoes, peeled and chopped*
*3cm (1½in) piece fresh ginger, julienned*
*3 pieces star anise*
*1 tablespoon chopped lemon grass*
*3 cups (750ml/24fl oz) water*
*2 teaspoons bean sauce*
*3 teaspoons lime juice*

Trim all the fat from the beef and slice the beef into strips 3mm (⅛in) thick. Cut zucchini (courgette) and carrot into 3cm (1½in) long thin strips.

Heat the oil in a wok or saucepan, brown the beef in 2 batches, drain on paper towels. To the same wok, add the garlic and onion, stir over heat until soft. Add the tomatoes, ginger, star anise and lemon grass, stir over heat for about 2 minutes or until aromatic. Return the beef to the wok, add the water, bring to the boil, simmer, covered for about 1 hour or until the beef is tender. Add the zucchini, carrot, bean sauce and lime juice, simmer for 1 minute, then serve immediately with some crusty bread rolls.

MAKES 2 LARGE SERVINGS

# Thai-Style Prawn Wonton Soup

If you prefer, you can buy ready-made wontons from the freezer section in Asian
food stores. Also, there are ready-made fish stocks available from supermarkets.

WONTONS
*500g (1lb) uncooked medium prawns*
*2 teaspoons sambal oelek*
*2 tablespoons chopped fresh coriander*
*2 tablespoons chopped lemon grass*
*200g (6$^{1}/_{2}$oz) packet gow gees pastry rounds*

PRAWN STOCK
*4 cups (1 litre/32fl oz) water*
*reserved prawn shells*
*2 kaffir lime leaves or 1 teaspoon grated lime zest*
*2 pieces dried galangal*
*2.5cm (1in) piece fresh ginger, sliced*

SOUP
*1 tablespoon oil*
*2 teaspoons shrimp paste*
*4 cups (1 litre/32fl oz) prepared prawn stock*
*or fish stock*
*1 small carrot, julienned*
*$^{1}/_{2}$ cup (60g/2oz) green peas*
*1 clove garlic, chopped*
*1 tablespoon lime juice*
*2 teaspoons Thai fish sauce*
*1 tablespoon chopped fresh coriander*

To make the wontons, peel and devein the prawns and
reserve the shells for the stock. Chop the prawns and
combine with the sambal oelek, coriander and lemon
grass in a bowl.

Make about 4 wontons at a time. Lay the pastry
rounds on a board, top with a teaspoon of the prawn
mixture, brush the edge of the rounds with water.

Gather the pastry round edges together and pinch
firmly to seal as shown. Set aside.

To make the prawn stock, combine the water,
reserved prawn shells, lime leaves, galangal and ginger
in a large saucepan. Bring to a boil then simmer for 15
minutes. Strain the liquid into a measuring jug and
make up to 4 cups (1 litre/32fl oz) with extra water if
it is needed.

To make the soup, heat the oil in a large saucepan,
add the shrimp paste and cook over low heat for 1
minute. Stir in the prepared prawn stock, carrot, peas,
garlic, lime juice and fish sauce. Bring to a boil and
simmer for 5 minutes.

Add the wontons and simmer for 5 minutes then
stir in the coriander. Serve immediately.

SERVES 4

Spoon a teaspoon of filling onto the gow gees pastry.

Gather the edges together and pinch firmly to seal.

*RIGHT: Thai-Style Prawn Wonton Soup*

# Kumara and Coconut Cream Soup

This is a deliciously creamy soup and is excellent for special occasions. If you prefer, you could use coconut milk instead of coconut cream to reduce the fat content.

1 tablespoon oil
1 small onion, finely chopped
$1/4$ teaspoon shrimp paste
$1/2$–1 small red chilli, chopped
1 tablespoon chopped lemon grass
250g (8oz) kumara (red sweet potato), peeled and chopped
$1^1/3$ cups (330ml/11fl oz) well-flavoured chicken stock
1 cup (250ml/8fl oz) coconut cream
3 teaspoons Thai fish sauce
6 large uncooked prawns, peeled and deveined
a handful of small fresh basil leaves

Process the oil, onion, shrimp paste, chilli and lemon grass until a paste consistency. Heat the paste in a large saucepan over low heat while stirring for about 5 minutes.

Add the kumara (red sweet potato), chicken stock, coconut cream and fish sauce. Cover and simmer the soup for 20 minutes.

Add the prawns and basil and simmer a further 3 minutes or until the prawns are just cooked.

MAKES 4 ENTREE SERVINGS OR
2 MAIN COURSE SERVINGS

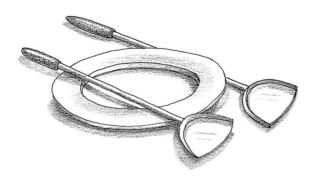

# Beef Meatball and Cucumber Soup

The meatballs can be prepared a day ahead or frozen, uncooked, to save time.

MEATBALLS
150g (5oz) minced beef
1 small onion, finely chopped
3 teaspoons good quality purchased or home-made green curry paste
1 tablespoon chopped lemon grass
SOUP
2 cups (500ml/16fl oz) well-flavoured beef stock
1 clove garlic, chopped
1 tablespoon chopped lemon grass
2cm ($3/4$in) piece fresh ginger, finely shredded
1 tablespoon Thai fish sauce
2 tablespoons lime juice
1 small green cucumber, peeled, seeded and finely sliced
60g (2oz) fresh or dried fine egg noodles
4 green shallots (spring onions), sliced

To make the meatballs, process the meatball ingredients together until combined. Evenly shape 2 teaspoons of the mixture into a ball, place on a plate then repeat shaping with the remaining mixture.

To make the soup, combine the stock, garlic, lemon grass, ginger, fish sauce and lime juice in a large saucepan. Bring to a boil, then simmer for 5 minutes.

Add the cucumber, noodles and meatballs then simmer for about 5 minutes or until the meatballs are cooked (they cook quickly). Add the green shallots (spring onions) before serving and top with a chopped red chilli if you would like extra spice.

MAKES 4 ENTREE SERVINGS OR 2 MAIN COURSE
SERVINGS

# Mixed Vegetable Soup

You can use any selection of vegetables in this recipe. I generally use a mixture of tiny broccoli florets, shredded red cabbage, quartered mini corn, straw mushrooms and green peas.

*1 tablespoon oil*
*1/4 teaspoon shrimp paste*
*1 clove garlic, finely chopped*
*2 coriander roots, finely chopped*
*4 green shallots (spring onions), chopped*
*3 cups (750ml/24fl oz) well-flavoured chicken or vegetable stock*
*1 cup (250ml/8fl oz) coconut milk*
*1 tablespoon Thai fish sauce*
*250g (8oz) mixture of chopped vegetables*
*2 tablespoons lime juice*
*2–4 teaspoons sambal oelek (to taste)*
*1 tablespoon chopped fresh coriander*

Heat the oil in a saucepan, add the shrimp paste, garlic, coriander roots and green shallots (spring onions). Cook gently for 1 minute.

Add the stock, coconut milk and fish sauce. Bring to a boil, add the vegetables and simmer for about 10 minutes or until the vegetables are only just tender. Stir in the lime juice, sambal oelek and coriander then serve immediately.

MAKES 4 ENTREE SERVINGS OR
2 MAIN COURSE SERVINGS

# Hot and Sour Chicken Soup

This soup is a variation of Tom Yum Khai and is made simple by using tom yum paste readily available from Asian food stores.

*3 cups (750ml/24fl oz) well-flavoured chicken stock*
*1–2 small green chillies, seeded and chopped*
*2 tablespoons finely chopped lemon grass*
*2 kaffir lime leaves or 1 teaspoon grated lime zest*
*3 teaspoons tom yum paste*
*1/2 cup (100g/3 1/2oz) drained canned straw mushrooms*
*1 chicken thigh fillet, thinly sliced*
*2 teaspoons Thai fish sauce*
*1 tablespoon lime juice*
*1 tablespoon chopped fresh coriander*
*2 green shallots (spring onions), sliced*

Combine the chicken stock, chillies, lemon grass, lime leaves, tom yum paste and mushrooms in a pan. Bring to a boil and then boil covered for 5 minutes.

Add the chicken, fish sauce and lime juice and simmer for about 3 minutes or until the chicken is cooked. Serve sprinkled with the coriander and green shallots (spring onions).

MAKES 4 ENTREE SERVINGS OR
2 MAIN COURSE SERVINGS

# Noodles and Rice

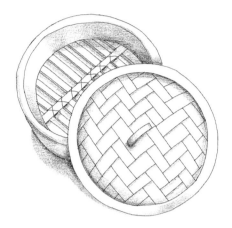

The varieties of noodles used in Asian cooking allows for a wonderful selection of simple dishes to make with all types of delicious additions. Rice is the most important food in any traditional Asian meal. Small portions of superbly flavoured dishes are served with the rice and are used to flavour the rice.

A typical meal will consist of three parts rice to two parts accompanying dishes. Always have plenty of steamed rice on hand to soak up the delicious sauces and juices.

Most of these rice and noodle dishes are quite filling and will serve up to four people as an accompaniment.

*RIGHT: Egg Noodle and Vegetable Stir-Fry*

# Egg Noodle and Vegetable Stir-Fry

If you don't like the unique flavour of Chinese dried mushrooms, omit them and double the quantity of the button mushrooms.

*6 Chinese dried mushrooms*
*150g (5oz) ribbon or thick fresh egg noodles*
*1 tablespoon oil*
*$^1/_4$ teaspoon sesame oil*
*45g ($1^1/_2$oz) fresh bean sprouts*
*1 small red capsicum (pepper), thinly sliced*
*1 small yellow capsicum (pepper), thinly sliced*
*75g ($2^1/_2$oz) button mushrooms, thinly sliced*
*$^1/_4$ cup (60ml/2fl oz) bottled Thai sweet chilli sauce*
*1 tablespoon light soy sauce*

Place the mushrooms in a bowl, pour over hot water to cover and stand for 20 minutes. Drain well. Cut the mushrooms into slices, discarding the tough stems.

Add the noodles to a large saucepan of boiling water, boil for 3 minutes then drain well, tossing in a little extra oil to stop the noodles from sticking together.

Heat the oils in a wok or large frying pan, add the bean sprouts, capsicums (peppers) and all the mushrooms, stir-fry until the capsicums are almost soft. Add the noodles and sauces, stir-fry until heated through and well combined.

SERVES 2 TO 4

# Steamed Jasmine Rice

This rice is the staple of Thai eating. The rice should be tender and moist enough to stick together without being gluggy. Use a saucepan that is large enough to have the rice and water mixture only about 2.5cm (1in) deep before cooking. This will bring the best results. Don't be tempted to lift the lid during the cooking or standing times – you will allow the heat and steam to escape.

*1 cup (200g/$6^1/_2$oz) jasmine rice*
*$2^1/_4$ cups (560ml/18fl oz) water*

Place the rice in a sieve and rinse under cold running water until the water runs clear; drain well. Place the rice and the water into a heavy-based saucepan. Stir over high heat until boiling then reduce the heat to a simmer, cover tightly with a lid and allow to simmer for 13 minutes without removing the lid.

Take the saucepan off the heat and stand for 10 minutes longer without removing the lid. When the time is up, remove the lid and stir the rice gently with a fork before serving.

SERVES 2 TO 4

VARIATIONS
◆ Toss through 3 tablespoons of chopped fresh coriander and $^1/_4$ small chopped red capsicum (pepper)
◆ Toss through 8 finely shredded English spinach leaves and $^1/_2$ teaspoon of sesame oil

# Thai Rice Balls

These rice balls can be deep-fried in hot oil if you prefer. I like the baking method as it is easy to pop them into the oven and let them cook by themselves.

*1 quantity Steamed Jasmine Rice*
*1 egg*
*¹/₂ cup chopped fresh coriander*
*1 tablespoon chopped lemon grass*
*1 teaspoon grated lime zest*
*2–4 teaspoons sambal oelek (to taste)*
*1 tablespoon Thai fish sauce*
*2 tablespoons chopped fresh basil*

Combine the rice, egg, coriander, lemon grass, lime zest, sambal oelek, fish sauce and basil in a bowl and mix well. Refrigerate the mixture for about 30 minutes or until cold. Lightly oil your hands and firmly roll 2–3 tablespoons of the mixture into a ball. Repeat with the remaining mixture.

Place the rice balls onto an oiled baking tray and bake in a 220°C (450°F) oven for about 20 minutes or until they are crisp and lightly browned on the outside. Serve with curries and stir-fries.

MAKES ABOUT 10

VARIATIONS
- Add 60g (2oz) finely chopped cooked prawns
- Add 60g (2oz) finely chopped ham
- Add 60g (2oz) flaked and well drained canned crab meat

---

*1 tablespoon Thai fish sauce*
*2 tablespoons lemon juice*
*2 teaspoons sugar*
*2 tablespoons chopped roasted peanuts*
*¹/₂ teaspoon chilli powder*
*4 green shallots (spring onions), chopped and fried until crisp*
*coriander leaves*

Place the noodles into a heatproof bowl, pour over enough boiling water to cover the noodles. Stand for 5 minutes then drain well, tossing through a little oil to stop the noodles from sticking together.

In the meantime, heat the oil in a wok or large frying pan and add the garlic, prawns and tofu, stir-fry until the prawns are just cooked. Add the noodles and combined sauces, juice, sugar, peanuts, chilli powder and green shallots (spring onions), then stir-fry over high heat until heated through. Serve sprinkled with coriander leaves.

SERVES 2 TO 4

# Rice and Shrimp Paste Omelette Rolls

These rolls are very flavoursome and are something different to serve for breakfast or brunch. Don't be put off by the strong smell of the shrimp paste. When it is cooked in a dish it adds a lovely typical Vietnamese flavour.

### RICE FILLING

*2 teaspoons oil*
*2 cloves garlic, crushed*
*2 teaspoons grated fresh ginger*
*1 small onion, finely chopped*
*½ teaspoon shrimp paste*
*1 tablespoon light soy sauce*
*1 cup (250ml/8fl oz) well-flavoured chicken stock*
*½ cup (125g/4oz) uncooked long-grain rice*

### OMELETTES

*2 tablespoons oil*
*8 green shallots (spring onions), chopped*
*2 small red chillies, seeded and finely chopped*
*5 eggs beaten*
*2 teaspoons fish sauce*
*½ cup (125ml/4fl oz) coconut cream*

To make the filling, heat the oil in a saucepan, add the garlic, ginger, onion and shrimp paste, stir over heat until aromatic. Add the soy sauce and stock to pan, bring to the boil. Add the rice, bring to the boil and boil for 1 minute. Reduce heat to medium, simmer for about 3 minutes or until nearly all the liquid has evaporated and holes appear through the rice.

Cover with a tight-fitting lid, reduce heat to lowest setting, cook for 20 minutes without removing the lid during this time. Remove from heat, stand for 10 minutes before fluffing with a fork or chopsticks.

To make the omelettes, heat half the oil in a 23cm (9in) omelette pan. Add half the green shallots (spring onions) and half the chillies, cook until the shallots turn a bright green and the mixture is aromatic.

Pour half the combined eggs, fish sauce and coconut cream, over the green shallots (spring onions) in the pan, swirling the pan so the egg mixture completely covers the base of the pan. Cook over a low heat until the omelette is just set.

Spoon half the rice filling into the centre of the omelette, fold over the sides to enclose, slide onto a plate. Keep warm while preparing the second omelette. Repeat the procedure to make the second omelette being sure the pan is well greased to avoid sticking.

SERVES 2

For the filling, simmer the rice until holes appear.

Cook the egg mixture until the omelette is just set.

*RIGHT: Rice and Shrimp Paste Omelette Rolls*

# Seafood and Fresh Rice Noodle Toss

Substitute any seafood such as scallops, crab or oysters.

*200g (6½oz) white fish fillet*
*8 fresh asparagus spears*
*200g (6½oz) uncooked prawns, peeled and deveined*
*1 tablespoon fish sauce*
*1 tablespoon rice vinegar*
*3 cloves garlic, crushed*
*¼ teaspoon freshly ground black pepper*
*200g (6½oz) fresh rice noodles*
*2 tablespoons oil*
*1 egg, lightly beaten*
*2 teaspoons fish sauce, extra*
*1 tablespoon oil, extra*
*1 tablespoon garlic chives*
*4 green shallots (spring onions), chopped*
*1 cup (80g/about 2½oz) bean sprouts*
*2 tablespoons roasted peanuts, chopped*
*1 small red chilli, sliced*
*1 quantity Fish Dipping Sauce (see THE*
*ESSENTIALS)*

Cut the fish fillet into 3cm (1¼in) pieces. Cut the asparagus diagonally into 4cm (1½in) lengths.

Combine the fish pieces, prawns, fish sauce, vinegar, garlic and pepper in a bowl. Refrigerate.

Add the rice noodles to a pan of boiling water, stand for 30 seconds. Drain, rinse under cold water.

Heat half the oil in a wok or frying pan until very hot, add the combined egg and extra fish sauce, swirl the pan to form a thin crêpe. Cook until just set. Carefully lift onto paper towels to drain. Roll up, cut into thin slices.

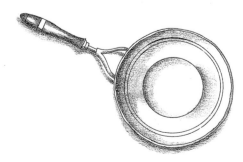

Heat the remaining oil in the same wok, add the seafood mixture, stir-fry until just cooked. Remove seafood from the wok, drain the liquid from the wok. Heat the extra oil in the same wok, add the garlic chives, green shallots (spring onions) and asparagus, stir-fry for 2 minutes. Return the seafood to the wok with the egg strips, noodles, bean sprouts and half the peanuts, stir-fry until well combined. Serve sprinkled with the remaining peanuts and chilli and drizzled with the Fish Dipping Sauce.

SERVES 2

# Cellophane Noodles and Chilli Vegetables

Any assortment of vegetables can be used in this recipe including red or green capsicums (peppers), pumpkin or swede, parsnip or turnip, instead of the ones I have suggested.

*50g (about 1½oz) cellophane noodles*
*2 Chinese dried mushrooms*
*200g (6½oz) daikon radish*
*1 small carrot*
*1 small green cucumber*
*1 stick celery, thinly sliced*
*4 green shallots (spring onions), sliced*
*¼ Chinese cabbage, finely shredded*
*1 tablespoon fresh mint leaves*
*2 tablespoons fresh coriander leaves*
*2 teaspoons toasted sesame seeds*
*1 teaspoon dried chilli flakes*
*DRESSING*
*3 cloves garlic, crushed*
*⅛ cup (80ml/2½fl oz) rice vinegar*
*2 tablespoons light soy sauce*
*3 teaspoons sesame oil*
*2 teaspoons fish sauce*

Cover the noodles with hot water in a bowl, stand 30 minutes, drain well. Cover the mushrooms with hot water in a small bowl, cover, stand 30 minutes. Remove and discard stems, slice mushrooms thinly.

Halve the radish lengthwise. Using a vegetable peeler, cut the radish and carrot into long thin ribbons. Run the teeth of a fork along the length of the cucumber, continuing all the way around then cut the cucumber into thin slices.

Combine the noodles, mushrooms, radish, carrot, cucumber, celery, green shallots (spring onions) cabbage, mint, coriander, sesame seeds and chilli flakes in a large bowl.

Make the dressing by combining the garlic, vinegar, soy sauce, sesame oil and fish sauce in a jar, shake well.

Just before serving, drizzle the dressing over the noodles and vegetables.

SERVES 2 TO 4

# Glutinous Rice with Beans and Sesame Seeds

This dish traditionally has a semi-sweet and slightly savoury flavour and is often eaten as a mid-morning or afternoon snack, but I have made it to be served as a savoury accompaniment. If you cannot find glutinous rice at your local Asian food store, cook plain steamed rice as directed in the following recipe.

*¾ cup (185g/6oz) glutinous rice*
*1½ cups (375ml/12fl oz) water*
*2 tablespoons oil*
*2 cloves garlic, crushed*
*2 teaspoons fish sauce*
*1 cup (250ml/8fl oz) well-flavoured chicken stock*
*2 cups (500ml/16fl oz) water, extra*
*¼ cup dried split yellow mung beans*
*2 teaspoons sesame seeds, toasted*
*1 tablespoon shredded coconut, toasted or*
*2 tablespoons roasted unsalted peanuts*

Soak the rice in plenty of cold water, stand for at least 8 hours or overnight. Drain, rinse and drain again.

Bring the water to the boil in a saucepan, add the rice, bring back to the boil and boil uncovered for 1 minute being careful that it doesn't boil over. Cover the pan with a lid and drain away as much liquid as possible. Return the pan to a low heat, cook, covered, for 20 minutes. Remove from heat, stand for 10 minutes before fluffing with a fork or chopsticks.

While the rice is cooking, prepare the mung bean topping. Heat the oil in a wok or saucepan, add the garlic, stir for 1 minute or until aromatic. Add the fish sauce, stock, extra water and the mung beans, simmer uncovered for about 20 minutes or until mung beans are tender and most of the liquid has evaporated, adding more water if necessary.

Transfer the rice to a plate, top with mung bean mixture, sprinkle with seeds and coconut or peanuts.

SERVES 2

# Steamed Rice

This is the method used to cook rice in the Vietnamese cuisine. To double the quantity of rice, the proportions are 2½ cups (625ml/20fl oz) cold water to 2 cups (500g/16oz) rice.

*1½ cups (375ml/12fl oz) cold water*
*1 cup (250g/8oz) long-grain rice or jasmine rice*

Bring the water to the boil in a medium heavy-based saucepan. Add the rice, bring back to the boil, boil for 1 minute, then reduce heat to medium and simmer for about 3 minutes or until most of the water has evaporated and holes appear through the rice. Reduce heat to lowest setting, or if you are using electric hotplates, have another hotplate already on lowest setting, cover pan with a tight fitting lid, cook over low heat for 20 minutes. Remove from heat, stand for 10 minutes before fluffing with a fork or chopsticks.

SERVES 2 TO 3

# Southern Fried Rice

This is a colourful and simple dish to make. It is excellent to serve with barbecues or as part of a buffet dinner. You can make the dish several hours ahead and reheat it, covered, in the oven or microwave oven quite successfully.

*2 tablespoons oil*
*1 small onion, thinly sliced*
*2 cloves garlic, crushed*
*1 tablespoon chopped lemon grass*
*$^{1}/_{2}$ teaspoon shrimp paste*
*1 small red capsicum (pepper), thinly sliced*
*150g (5oz) green beans, chopped*
*2 cups (about 400g/12$^{1}/_{2}$oz) cooked long-grain rice*
*1 tablespoon light soy sauce*
*2 teaspoons Thai fish sauce*
*2–4 teaspoons sambal oelek (to taste)*
*3 tablespoons chopped fresh coriander*

Heat the oil in a wok or large frying pan, add the onion, garlic, lemon grass, shrimp paste, capsicum (pepper) and beans. Cook the mixture gently until the onion is soft.

Add the rice and stir-fry until it is heated through. Add the remaining ingredients and stir-fry over high heat until well combined.

SERVES 2 TO 4

VARIATION

Any vegetables can be used in this dish, such as broccoli, asparagus or carrot sticks

# Fresh Rice Noodles in Thai Sauce

If the fresh rice noodles are not available, you can use dried rice stick noodles instead. Follow the same method.

*200g (6$^{1}/_{2}$oz) fresh thick rice noodles*
*2 tablespoons oil*
*2 cloves garlic, crushed*
*3 teaspoons good quality purchased or home-made red curry paste*
*1 tablespoon chopped lemon grass*
*6 green shallots (spring onions), chopped*
*150g (5oz) can coconut cream*
*1 tablespoon Thai fish sauce*

Place the noodles in a heatproof bowl and pour over enough boiling water to cover the noodles. Stand for 10 minutes then drain well, tossing through a little oil to stop the noodles from sticking together.

Heat the oil in a wok, add the garlic, curry paste, lemon grass and green shallots (spring onions), cook gently until the green shallots are soft. Add the coconut cream, fish sauce and noodles and toss gently until heated through.

SERVES 2 TO 4

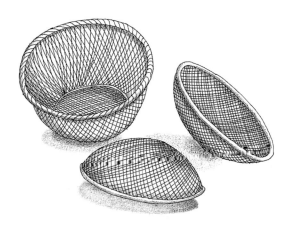

*LEFT: Southern Fried Rice*

# Rice Noodles with Chicken and Capsicum

Rice stick noodles are dried noodles that do not require cooking, all they require is a soak in hot water.

*180g (6oz) rice stick noodles*
*2 tablespoons oil*
*2 single chicken breast fillets, sliced*
*1 small red capsicum (pepper), thinly sliced*
*1 small green capsicum (pepper), thinly sliced*
*2 cloves garlic, crushed*
*2 tablespoons chopped lemon grass*
*1 tablespoon grated fresh ginger*
*1 tablespoon oyster sauce*
*2 teaspoons Thai fish sauce*
*1 tablespoon chopped roasted peanuts*

Place the noodles in a heatproof bowl, cover with boiling water, stand for 5 minutes then drain well, tossing through a little oil to stop the noodles from sticking together.

Heat the oil in a wok or large frying pan, add the chicken and stir-fry until lightly browned and just cooked then remove from the wok.

Add the capsicums (peppers), garlic, lemon grass and ginger to the wok, stir-fry until the capsicums are tender. Add the noodles, chicken and sauces and stir-fry over high heat until heated through. Sprinkle with the peanuts and serve hot.

SERVES 2 TO 4

# Bean Thread Vermicelli with Lime, Cucumber and Orange

You can also use regular vermicelli pasta in this recipe. It will give a different appearance to the final dish as bean thread vermicelli noodles become translucent when prepared.

*100g (3¹/₂oz) bean thread vermicelli noodles*
*1 tablespoon oil*
*2 cloves garlic, crushed*
*1 tablespoon chopped lemon grass*
*¹/₄ teaspoon chilli powder*
*1 small (200g/6¹/₂oz) green cucumber, finely sliced*
*2 teaspoons Thai fish sauce*
*3 teaspoons sugar*
*2 tablespoons lime juice*
*1 orange, segmented*

Place the vermicelli in a heatproof bowl and cover with boiling water. Stand for 5 minutes, cut into 2.5cm (1in) lengths using a pair of scissors then drain well.

Heat the oil in a wok or large frying pan, add the garlic, lemon grass, chilli powder and cucumber and stir-fry until the cucumber is just softened. Add the fish sauce, sugar and lime juice and toss well. Add the noodles and orange segments and toss gently until heated through.

SERVES 2 TO 4

# Chilli and Coconut Rice

This dish is a richly-flavoured rice accompaniment for curries and stir-fries.

*1 tablespoon oil*
*1 clove garlic, chopped*
*1 small onion, finely chopped*
*$^1/_2$ teaspoon shrimp paste*
*1 cup (200g/6$^1/_2$oz) jasmine rice*
*1$^1/_2$ cups (375ml/12fl oz) well-flavoured chicken stock*
*$^3/_4$ cup (185ml/6fl oz) coconut milk*
*2 medium red chillies, seeded and chopped*
*2 tablespoons shredded fresh basil*

Heat the oil in a heavy-based saucepan, add the garlic, onion and shrimp paste. Cook gently, stirring often, for several minutes or until the onion is very soft.

Meanwhile, place the rice in a sieve and rinse thoroughly under cold running water until the water runs clear then drain well.

Add the rice, stock and coconut milk to the onion mixture in the saucepan and stir well. Bring to a boil while stirring then reduce the heat to a simmer. Cover tightly and simmer for 13 minutes without removing the lid. Remove from the heat and stand for a further 10 minutes without removing the lid.

Use a fork to toss through the chillies and basil just before serving.

SERVES 2 TO 4

# Brown Rice with Tofu and Ginger

*1 cup (200g/6$^1/_2$oz) brown rice*
*1 tablespoon oil*
*$^1/_2$ teaspoon sesame oil*
*1 tablespoon grated fresh ginger*
*2 cloves garlic, crushed*
*2 tablespoons chopped lemon grass*
*1 zucchini (courgette), grated*
*100g (3$^1/_2$oz) firm tofu, cubed*
*1 tablespoon light soy sauce*
*1 tablespoon oyster sauce*
*3 tablespoons chopped fresh mint*

Add the rice to a large saucepan of boiling water, boil uncovered for 30 minutes then drain well.

Heat the oils in a wok or large frying pan, add the ginger, garlic and lemon grass and cook gently for 1 minute. Add the zucchini (courgette) and tofu and stir-fry gently until the zucchini is soft. Add the rice, sauces and mint and stir-fry until heated through.

SERVES 2 TO 4

VARIATIONS

◆ Add 60g (2oz) of cooked cubed fish fillet and 2 tablespoons of chopped fresh coriander before serving
◆ Stir through 60g (2oz) roast beef strips and 1 chopped red chilli before serving

# Wonton Noodle Strips with Eggplant and Capsicum

This colourful combination can be served warm as an accompaniment or,
as a light lunch dish or, as a cold salad.

*1 small eggplant (aubergine)*
*oil*
*1 red capsicum (pepper), quartered*
*100g (3¹/₂oz) x 9cm (3¹/₂in) square or round wonton wrappers, halved*
*1 tablespoon oil*
*3 cloves garlic, thinly sliced*
*4 green shallots (spring onions), cut into short lengths*
*1–2 medium red chillies, shredded*
*3 teaspoons Thai fish sauce*
*¹/₄ teaspoon sesame oil*
*1 tablespoon shredded fresh basil*

Cut the eggplant (aubergine) into thin slices, brush with oil and grill until browned and soft. Cut the eggplant slices into wide strips.

Grill the capsicum (pepper) skin side up until the skin blackens and blisters. Place the capsicum into a paper bag then cool.

Peel away and discard the capsicum skin and cut the capsicum into thick slices.

Add the wonton wrappers to a large saucepan of boiling water, boil for 3 minutes then drain, tossing with a little extra oil to prevent the wrappers from sticking together.

Heat the tablespoon of oil in a wok or large frying pan, add the garlic, green shallots (spring onions) and chillies, cook gently until the shallots are soft. Add the eggplant, capsicum, wonton wrappers, fish sauce and sesame oil, stir-fry, tossing gently until heated through and well combined. Sprinkle with the basil and serve while hot.

SERVES 2 TO 4

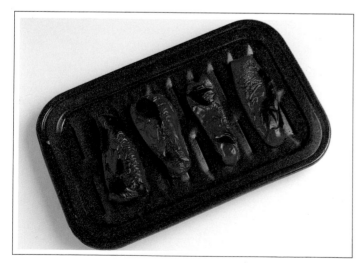

Grill the capsicum skin side up until the skin blackens and blisters.

Peel away and discard the skin and cut the capsicum into thick slices.

*RIGHT: Wonton Noodle Strips with Eggplant and Capsicum*

# Beef, Tomato and Bamboo with Rice

*1 tablespoon oil*
*350g (11oz) lean beef mince*
*3 cloves garlic, crushed*
*2 leeks, chopped*
*2 ripe tomatoes, finely chopped*
*1 parsnip, chopped*
*1 stick celery, chopped*
*1/3 cup (80g/2 1/2oz) uncooked long-grain rice*
*1 tablespoon fish sauce*
*1 cup (250ml/8fl oz) well-flavoured beef stock*
*1 x 227g (7oz) can sliced bamboo shoots, drained*
*2 tablespoons chopped fresh mint*

Heat the oil in a wok or saucepan, add the mince, stir-fry until well browned and dry. Add the garlic, leeks, tomatoes, parsnip, celery and rice, stir-fry quickly for about 2 minutes or until well combined.

Add the fish sauce and beef stock, bring to the boil and boil uncovered for about 3 minutes or until most of the liquid has evaporated and holes appear through the rice. Reduce heat to low, or if using electric hotplates, transfer to another hotplate already on lowest setting, cover, cook for 15 minutes without uncovering during this cooking time. Stir through the bamboo shoots and mint before serving.

SERVES 2

# Minted Rice with Chicken in Tomato Sauce

A quick and easy method with chicken mince or pork mince. The sauce can be made a day ahead and reheated close to serving.

*1 1/2 cups (375ml/12fl oz) water*
*1 cup (250g/8oz) uncooked long-grain rice*
*1/4 cup chopped fresh mint*
*1 tablespoon oil*
*250g (8oz) chicken mince*
*3 cloves garlic, crushed*
*1 onion, finely chopped*
*2 ripe tomatoes, finely chopped*
*3/4 cup (185ml/6fl oz) well-flavoured chicken stock*
*2 teaspoons fish sauce*
*2 teaspoons tomato paste*
*1/4 teaspoon dried chilli flakes*

Bring the water to the boil in a medium heavy-based pan, add the rice, bring back to the boil and boil uncovered for 1 minute. Reduce heat to medium, simmer uncovered for about 3 minutes or until all of the liquid has evaporated and holes appear through the rice. Cover with a tight-fitting lid, reduce heat to low, or if using electric hotplates, transfer to another hotplate already on lowest setting and cook for a further 20 minutes. Remove from the heat, stand covered for 10 minutes before removing the lid and fluffing with a fork or chopsticks. Toss through the mint. Keep warm.

Heat the oil in a wok or saucepan, add the mince, cook, stirring and breaking up any lumps, until dry and changed in colour. Add the garlic, onion and tomatoes, cook, stirring until aromatic and the tomatoes have softened.

Add the chicken stock, fish sauce, tomato paste and chilli flakes, bring to the boil, simmer covered for 7 minutes. Serve with the minted rice.

SERVES 2

# Lamb and Spinach with Soft Rice Noodles

Use any type of leafy greens such as bok choy, choy sum, chicory or silverbeet (Swiss chard).

300g (10oz) lamb fillet or beef skirt steak
2 teaspoons fish sauce
1/2 teaspoon freshly ground black pepper
200g (6 1/2oz) fresh rice noodles
10 leaves English spinach
100g (3 1/2oz) green beans
1 tablespoon sesame oil
4 cloves garlic, crushed
1 onion, cut into 8 wedges
4 golden shallots (brown shallots), halved
5 yellow tear drop tomatoes, halved
1 tablespoon light soy sauce
1 tablespoon oyster sauce
1 tablespoon fish sauce, extra
1 tablespoon chopped fresh garlic chives
1/4 cup (60ml/2fl oz) water
2 tablespoons chopped fresh coriander

Cut the lamb into thin strips. Combine the lamb with the fish sauce and pepper in a small bowl, cover, refrigerate while preparing the remaining ingredients.

Cover the noodles with boiling water, stand for 30 seconds, drain. Cut the spinach into thick shreds about 5cm (2in) wide. Cut the green beans into 4cm (1 1/2in) lengths.

Heat the sesame oil in a wok or large frying pan, add the noodles and garlic, stir-fry for about 2 minutes or until aromatic and the noodles start to brown, transfer to a serving plate.

Reheat the same wok, add the lamb mixture, stir-fry for 1 minute, add onion and golden shallots (brown shallots), stir-fry a further 2 minutes. Add beans, stir-fry for 2 minutes then add spinach, tomatoes, sauces, chives and water, stir-fry until spinach is just wilted. Return noodles to pan with coriander, toss well.

SERVES 2

# Chicken and Rice Casserole

'Lovely legs' are chicken drumsticks without the skin and with the bottom part of the drumstick cut off.

3 Chinese dried mushrooms
4 cups (1 litre/32fl oz) water
2 chicken thigh cutlets, skin removed
2 chicken drumsticks or 'lovely legs', skin removed
1 tablespoon oil
3 cloves garlic, crushed
1 onion, finely chopped
1/2 cup (125g/4oz) long-grain rice
2 teaspoons light soy sauce
2 teaspoons fish sauce
1/4 teaspoon freshly ground black pepper
3 green shallots (spring onions), chopped
1 tablespoon chopped fresh coriander
1 small red chilli, seeded and finely chopped

Cover the mushrooms with hot water in a bowl, stand 30 minutes, drain. Discard the tough stems, thinly slice the mushrooms.

Bring the water to a boil in a medium saucepan. Add the chicken pieces, bring back to the boil and simmer, covered for 25 minutes. Remove the chicken and reserve 1 1/2 cups (375ml/12fl oz) of the stock.

Heat the oil in a wok or large saucepan, add the chicken, cook until browned all over, turning during cooking. Drain on paper towels. To the same wok, add the garlic and onion, cook, stirring for about 1 minute or until aromatic. Add the rice, stir-fry over high heat for about 2 minutes or until just browned. Add the reserved chicken stock, soy sauce, fish sauce, mushrooms and pepper, boil, uncovered for 6 minutes or until most of the liquid has evaporated.

Place the chicken pieces on top of the rice, cover the wok, reduce heat to low, cook for a further 15 minutes without removing the lid during cooking. Toss through the green shallots (spring onions), coriander and chilli before serving.

SERVES 2 TO 4

# Pork and Coconut Curry with Noodles and Sprouts

*500g (16oz) pork neck*
*3 spring (bulb) onions*
*1 tablespoon oil*
*2 tablespoons chopped lemon grass*
*3 cloves garlic, crushed*
*1 tablespoon curry powder*
*1/4 teaspoon chilli powder*
*1 3/4 cups (435ml/14fl oz) water*
*1 cup (250ml/8fl oz) well-flavoured chicken stock*
*2 medium potatoes, peeled and quartered*
*100g (3 1/2oz) baby yellow squash, quartered*
*2 teaspoons cornflour*
*2 teaspoons fish sauce*
*1/2 cup (125ml/4fl oz) coconut cream*
*125g (4oz) bundle fresh thin egg noodles, cut into thirds*
*1/4 cup (30g/1oz) mung bean sprouts*
*coriander and chillies for garnish*

Trim any excess fat from the pork, cut the pork into 4cm (1 1/2in) pieces. Cut the tender green tops of the spring onions into 2cm (3/4in) sections, halve the bulbs.

Heat the oil in a wok or frying pan, cook pork in batches until browned, drain on paper towels. Drain away excess oil from wok, reserving about 2 teaspoons.

Add the lemon grass, garlic, curry powder and chilli powder to the wok, cook, stirring for 1 minute or until aromatic. Return the pork to the wok with water and chicken stock, bring to the boil, reduce heat and simmer covered for 20 minutes. Add spring onions, potatoes and squash, simmer, covered for 20 minutes.

Stir in the cornflour blended with the fish sauce and coconut cream, then add the noodles, simmer covered for 5 minutes. Serve sprinkled with the chopped coriander and chilli strips with the mung bean sprouts on the side.

SERVES 2 TO 4

# Crisp Noodles and Alfalfa

I have avoided deep-fried foods in this book and have looked for healthy alternatives, but for this recipe I couldn't resist deep-frying the rice vermicelli to obtain that wonderful crispy texture that makes this dish so delicious. You may use any leftover cooked meats instead of the chicken and prawns, and if you can't find black sesame seeds at your local Asian food store, toast some white sesame seeds and use those instead.

*oil for deep-frying*
*100g (3 1/2oz) rice vermicelli*
*1/4 cup (15g/1/2oz) alfalfa sprouts*
*100g (3 1/2oz) cooked chicken, chopped*
*8 large cooked prawns, peeled and chopped*
*8 cherry tomatoes, halved*
*1 tablespoon chopped fresh coriander*
*1 tablespoon chopped fresh mint*
*1 tablespoon black sesame seeds*
DRESSING
*1/4 cup (60ml/2fl oz) oil*
*1 small red chilli, seeded and finely chopped*
*1 tablespoon grated fresh ginger*
*1 1/2 tablespoons fish sauce*
*1/4 cup (60ml/2fl oz) lime juice*
*2 teaspoons sesame oil*
*2 teaspoons honey*

Heat the oil in deep-fryer or large saucepan until hot, add the rice vermicelli in 2 batches, it will quickly turn white and puff up, remove from the pan with a slotted spoon, drain on paper towels. Place on a serving plate.

Make the dressing by combining all the dressing ingredients in a screw-top jar, shake well.

Serve the rice vermicelli with the alfalfa, chicken, prawns, tomatoes, coriander, mint and sesame seeds and drizzled with the dressing just before serving.

SERVES 2 TO 4

*RIGHT: From top: Pork and Coconut Curry with Noodles and Sprouts; Crisp Noodles and Alfalfa*

# Main Courses

This section has been planned with all styles of eating in mind. There is a great variety of dishes from the traditional to the elegant and some are more appropriate for family fare. In a traditional Asian meal, the meat, fish or poultry would not be the main feature but is served to accompany and flavour the rice. Serve one main course for every two people at an Asian meal with a large quantity of steamed rice, a soup, a vegetable dish and a noodle or rice dish. All the dishes would be placed in the centre and everyone helps themselves. The main courses in this section serve two on their own, or some will serve four as part of an Asian meal.

*RIGHT: Chilli Garlic Quail with Ginger*

## Chilli Garlic Quail with Ginger

Although a little fiddly to eat, quail are absolutely delicious smothered with a hot chilli marinade and baked, grilled or barbecued to perfection. Use less sambal oelek for a milder flavour.

*4–6 quail*
*3 cloves garlic, crushed*
*1 small onion, grated*
*3 tablespoons sambal oelek*
*1 tablespoon light soy sauce*
*2 teaspoons grated fresh ginger*
*2 teaspoons brown sugar*
*1 tablespoon oil*

Using a sharp pair of kitchen scissors, cut the quail in half, cutting away and discarding the backbones and necks (if attached). It is easier to use the scissors than a sharp knife as you have a little more control over cutting through the bones.

Combine all the remaining ingredients in a bowl and mix well. Using a pastry brush, brush the mixture generously over the pieces of quail. Place the quail in a non-aluminium dish and pour over any remaining marinade. Cover the quail and refrigerate for at least 4 hours or overnight is even better to allow the flavours to develop.

Place the quail in a single layer, skin side up, on a wire rack over a baking dish. Bake in a 190°C (375°F) oven, brushing with any marinade remaining in the dish, for about 30 minutes or until the quail are cooked through.

SERVES 2 TO 4

VARIATION
Chicken legs or thighs can be cooked using this marinade. They would take about 40 minutes to cook through

## Thai Green Curry Chicken

There are many variations of green curry chicken. This version uses a good quality purchased curry paste. Buy it from the supermarket or an Asian food store.

*375g (12oz) chicken thigh fillets*
*2 tablespoons oil*
*2 cloves garlic, crushed*
*1 teaspoon shrimp paste*
*1 tablespoon good quality purchased or home-made green curry paste*
*1 tablespoon chopped lemon grass*
*2 kaffir lime leaves or 1 teaspoon grated lime zest*
*1 tablespoon Thai fish sauce*
*1/2 cup (125ml/4fl oz) water*
*1/2 cup (125ml/4fl oz) coconut cream*
*1/2 cup (60g/2oz) peas*
*200g (6 1/2oz) broccoli, cut into florets*
*2 tablespoons fresh coriander leaves*
*1 tablespoon shredded fresh basil*

Cut any excess fat from the chicken fillets, then cut the fillets in half. Heat the oil in a wok or large frying pan, add the chicken a handful at a time and cook until browned all over. Remove from the wok and drain on paper towels.

Add the garlic, shrimp paste and curry paste to the wok and cook gently for a few seconds. Stir in the lemon grass, lime leaves, fish sauce, water and coconut cream. Bring to a boil, add the chicken pieces and simmer for 10 minutes, partially covered.

Add the peas and broccoli and simmer for a further 5 minutes. Stir in the coriander and basil then serve immediately with Steamed Jasmine Rice.

SERVES 2 TO 4

# Braised Chicken Drumsticks

I always prefer to remove the skin and fat from chicken if it is in a braise such as this. The chicken is delicious to eat to the last mouthful.

2 cloves garlic, chopped
1 small onion, chopped
1–2 red chillies, seeded and chopped
$^1/_4$ teaspoon ground cumin
$^1/_4$ teaspoon ground coriander
$^1/_4$ teaspoon ground turmeric
$^1/_4$ teaspoon five spice powder
1 teaspoon shrimp paste
6 chicken drumsticks
2 tablespoons oil
$^1/_2$ cup (125ml/4fl oz) well-flavoured chicken stock
$^1/_2$ cup (125ml/4fl oz) coconut milk
1 tablespoon chopped fresh coriander

Process the garlic, onion, chillies, cumin, coriander, turmeric, five spice powder and shrimp paste until a paste consistency. Remove the skin and any fat from the chicken. Heat the oil in a wok or large frying pan, add the chicken and cook until browned all over then remove from the wok.

Add the paste to the wok and cook gently for 1 minute. Add the chicken, stock and coconut milk. Cover the wok and simmer for about 30 minutes or until the chicken is cooked through, stirring and turning the chicken occasionally. Sprinkle with the coriander and serve with rice or noodles.

SERVES 2 TO 4

# Stir-Fried Chicken and Asparagus

If you cannot find good fresh asparagus, substitute green beans or snow peas (mangetout).

4 chicken thigh fillets
1 tablespoon oil
12 spears fresh asparagus, cut into short lengths
2 cloves garlic, crushed
$^1/_4$ teaspoon shrimp paste
$^1/_2$ teaspoon grated fresh ginger
2 medium fresh red chillies, finely chopped
1 teaspoon light soy sauce
3 teaspoons Thai fish sauce
2 tablespoons well-flavoured chicken stock
$^1/_2$ cup (15g/$^1/_2$oz) shredded fresh basil

Remove any fat from the chicken. Cut the chicken into thin slices. Heat the oil in a wok or large frying pan, add the chicken and asparagus. Stir-fry until the chicken is almost cooked. Add the garlic, shrimp paste, ginger and chillies, stir-fry for a few seconds.

Stir in the soy sauce, fish sauce and stock then stir until boiling and well combined. Gently toss through the basil then serve immediately.

SERVES 2 TO 4

# Spicy Roasted Duck Breast Rolls

This dish can look very impressive at a dinner party and is very easy to prepare.
The spices go well with the duck, but if duck is unavailable, substitute chicken
breast fillets.

Terracotta platter with shell inlay from Corso de Fiori

*2 single duck breasts*
*1 tablespoon roasted peanuts, finely ground*
*2 green shallots (spring onions), finely chopped*
*1 teaspoon grated fresh ginger*
*2 teaspoons chopped fresh coriander*
*2 cloves garlic, crushed*
*2 teaspoons grated fresh ginger, extra*
*½ teaspoon five spice powder*
*½ teaspoon ground cinnamon*
*1 tablespoon honey*
*1 teaspoon tomato paste*
*½ teaspoon freshly ground black pepper*
*1 tablespoon light soy sauce*
*1 teaspoon sesame oil*
*2 cloves garlic, sliced, extra*
*10 leaves choy sum, halved*
*75g (2½oz) oyster mushrooms,*
*¼ cup (60ml/2fl oz) water*

Cut away and discard the duck wing by cutting
through the joint. Carefully run a sharp knife along
breast bone of duck, continue with short cuts until
the meat comes away from the bone. Remove the skin
from the breast fillet. Repeat with other duck breast.
With the flat side of a knife, or with a meat mallet,
flatten out each breast until about 1cm (½in) thick.

Combine the peanuts, green shallots (spring
onions), ginger and coriander in a bowl. Divide the
peanut mixture between each duck breast, spread
evenly over the surface. Roll up the duck breasts tightly
from a short end to form a roll, secure with toothpicks.
Brush with the combined garlic, extra ginger, spices,
honey, tomato paste, pepper and soy sauce. Reserve
about 1½ tablespoons of this baste for the vegetables.
Place the duck rolls on a baking tray, bake in a 180°C
(350°F) oven for about 35 minutes or until cooked,
brushing during cooking with any remaining baste.

Meanwhile, heat the sesame oil in a wok or frying
pan, add the extra garlic and reserved baste, stir for
about 1 minute or until aromatic. Add the choy sum,
mushrooms and water, stir-fry until the choy sum is
just wilted. Slice the rolls and serve with the vegetables.

SERVES 2

Cutting along the breast bone to remove the meat
from the bone.

Rolling the duck breast up tightly from a short end.

*RIGHT: Spicy Roasted Duck Breast Rolls*

# Grilled Lemon Grass and Chilli Chicken

The lemon grass and chilli give this dish a very fresh and spicy flavour and it tastes especially good eaten with some of the Pickled Carrot, Daikon Radish and Cucumber (see SALADS AND VEGETABLES). I have used the Shallot Oil that I store in my pantry, for extra flavour, but you can use vegetable oil instead.

*1 tablespoon lime juice*
*1 tablespoon chopped lemon grass*
*1 tablespoon grated fresh ginger*
*1 teaspoon red chilli flakes*
*1 onion, grated*
*2 cloves garlic, crushed*
*1 tablespoon sugar*
*1 tablespoon fish sauce*
*2 chicken thigh cutlets*
*2 chicken drumsticks*
*2 tablespoons Shallot Oil (see THE ESSENTIALS)*

Using a blender or mortar and pestle, blend the lime juice, lemon grass, ginger, chilli flakes, onion, garlic, sugar and fish sauce until a smooth paste.

Remove the skin from the chicken. Make 2 cuts into each piece of chicken at the thickest part. Brush the paste all over the chicken pieces and into the cuts, cover and refrigerate 3 hours or overnight to allow the flavours to develop. Cut 2 pieces of foil into 16cm (6½in) squares. Place a cutlet and a drumstick in the centre of each piece of the foil, fold up the ends to form a parcel. Place the parcels on a baking tray and bake in a 190°C (375°F) oven for 30 minutes. Open the parcels then bake for a further 30 minutes or until the chicken is tender, brushing with the Shallot Oil during cooking to prevent it from drying out.

SERVES 2

# Baked Chicken Strips with Ginger and Tomato

This is a very light and healthy dish best served with lots of steamed rice to soak up the delicious juices.

*2 Chinese dried mushrooms*
*200g (6½oz) chicken thigh fillets*
*3cm (1½in) piece fresh ginger*
*4 leaves choy sum or English spinach, finely shredded*
*3 green shallots (spring onions), chopped*
*2 medium ripe tomatoes, chopped*
*1 tablespoons tomato paste*
*1 tablespoon fish sauce*

Soak the mushrooms in hot water for 30 minutes. Remove and discard the stems, slice thinly.

Cut the chicken into 5mm (¼in) thick strips. Cut the ginger into long thin strips. Boil or steam the choy sum until just wilted, refresh under cold water, drain.

Combine the mushrooms, chicken, ginger, green shallots (spring onions), tomatoes, paste and sauce in a 5 cup (1¼litres/40fl oz) capacity ovenproof dish, bake in a 180°C (350°F) oven about 45 minutes or until the chicken is cooked. Stir in the choy sum. Serve with steamed rice.

SERVES 2 TO 4

VARIATIONS
- In place of the chicken, use lean pork or lamb cut into strips
- Fish fillets such as snapper or perch, cut into large pieces, can be substituted for the chicken. Just reduce the cooking time to 30 minutes or until the fish is cooked, and add 1 tablespoon of lime juice at the end of the cooking time

# Barbecued Chicken Livers and Potato Scallops

Something perfect for a barbecue, you can serve the livers as appetisers or as a main meal with the potatoes as I have suggested, and perhaps with the Grapefruit, Sprout and Cucumber Salad (see SALADS AND VEGETABLES). You can prepare the livers ahead of time.

*1 tablespoon grated fresh ginger*
*4 cloves garlic, crushed*
*2 tablespoons sweet chilli sauce*
*350g (11oz) chicken livers, trimmed*
*2 medium potatoes*
*2 tablespoons fresh coriander leaves*
*1 quantity Fish Dipping Sauce (see THE ESSENTIALS)*

Combine the ginger, garlic and sauce in a bowl, add the chicken livers, stir until well coated. Cover and, refrigerate 1 hour.

If you are using new potatoes, scrub them well and do not peel them. Cut into 5mm (¼in) thick slices.

Barbecue or grill the livers and potatoes over medium heat until browned and cooked through. Sprinkle the livers with the coriander leaves and serve with Fish Dipping Sauce.

SERVES 2

VARIATION
You can use quartered chicken breast fillets, or lamb cutlets in place of the livers if you prefer

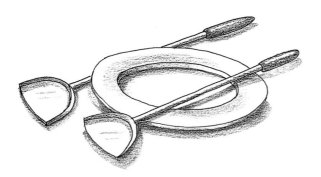

# Roasted Honey Spiced Quail

These quail are best eaten with your fingers and you may find that just one quail each is not enough, so double the recipe if you have a big appetite. They are just as delicious eaten cold and served with the Vegetable Platter with a Dipping Sauce (see SALADS AND VEGETABLES).

*2 quail*
*3 green shallots (spring onions), finely chopped*
*1 tablespoon grated fresh ginger*
*3 cloves garlic, crushed*
*pinch chilli powder*
*2 tablespoons honey*
*2 tablespoons light soy sauce*
*1 tablespoon rice vinegar*
*crushed coriander seeds for sprinkling, optional*

Using sharp kitchen scissors, cut the quail on either side of the backbone and open out flat. Tuck the wings behind the breast bones.

With a mortar and pestle, grind the green shallots (spring onions), ginger, garlic and chilli powder together until the mixture forms a paste. Combine the paste with the honey, soy sauce and vinegar in a shallow dish, mix well. Add the quail, spooning the marinade over the quail. Cover and refrigerate overnight to allow the flavours to develop.

Place the quail breast side up on a wire rack in a baking dish. Add some water to the baking dish to prevent the juices burning during cooking. Bake the quail in a 190°C (375°F) oven for about 30 minutes or until cooked through, basting frequently during cooking with any remaining marinade. Sprinkle with crushed coriander seeds before serving.

SERVES 2

~ Tip ~
A simple way to crush the coriander seeds is by grinding them in short bursts in an electric coffee grinder. Otherwise, a blender or mortar and pestle also work well.

# Chicken Noodle Lettuce Cups

2 single chicken breast fillets
2 teaspoons dark soy sauce
1 teaspoon fish sauce
75g (2½oz) rice vermicelli
2 tablespoons oil
8 choy sum leaves or English spinach leaves
4 mignonette lettuce leaves
1 small carrot, julienned
1 tablespoon shredded fresh coriander leaves
1 tablespoon shredded fresh mint leaves
1 tablespoon roasted peanuts, chopped

DRESSING
1 small red chilli, seeded and finely chopped
2 cloves garlic, crushed
1 tablespoon honey
1 tablespoon rice vinegar
2 tablespoons lime juice
2 tablespoons fish sauce
2 tablespoons water

Combine the chicken, soy sauce and fish sauce in a bowl, cover and refrigerate overnight.

Cover the rice vermicelli with boiling water in a bowl, stand 30 minutes. Drain well then cut into short lengths.

Heat some of the oil in a wok or pan, add the choy sum, stir-fry until just wilted, add the rice vermicelli, stir until combined. Spoon some of this mixture into each lettuce leaf. Sprinkle with carrot.

Make the dressing by combining all the dressing ingredients in a jar, shake well.

Heat the remaining oil in a wok, add the chicken, cook for about 8 minutes or until well browned on both sides and cooked through. Slice the chicken thinly, arrange over the rice vermicelli mixture in lettuce cups. Sprinkle with the coriander, mint and peanuts, drizzle with the dressing.

SERVES 2

# Chicken Curry with Carrot and Parsnip

2 tablespoons chopped lemon grass
4 cloves garlic, crushed
1 small onion, grated
1 small red chilli, chopped
1 tablespoon good quality purchased red curry paste
1 tablespoon curry powder
2 teaspoons shrimp paste
1 single chicken breast, on the bone, skin removed
2 chicken thighs, skin removed
2 tablespoons oil
1 large onion, cut into 8 wedges, extra
1 large ripe tomato, chopped
1½ cups (375ml/12fl oz) well-flavoured chicken stock
½ cup (125ml/4fl oz) water
1 tablespoon fish sauce
1 carrot, chopped
1 parsnip, chopped
⅔ cup (165ml/5½fl oz) coconut milk
1 tablespoon roasted peanuts, chopped
1 fresh green chilli, chopped

Blend the lemon grass, garlic, onion, red chilli, curry paste, curry powder and shrimp paste until smooth. Using a sharp knife or cleaver, cut the chicken breast in half. Make 2 cuts into the thighs at the thickest part. Brush half the curry paste all over chicken pieces and into the cuts, cover, stand for 1 hour.

Heat some oil in a wok or pan, brown the chicken in batches, adding extra oil as needed. Drain on paper towels. Drain excess oil from wok, add remaining curry paste, cook until aromatic. Add extra onion and tomato, stir-fry for 3 minutes or until tomato is soft.

Add chicken thighs, stock and water, simmer, uncovered 30 minutes. Add fish sauce, breast pieces, carrot and parsnip, simmer, uncovered 30 minutes or until chicken is cooked. Stir in coconut milk, bring to the boil. Serve sprinkled with the peanuts and chilli.

SERVES 2

*LEFT: From left: Chicken Noodle Lettuce Cups;*
*Chicken Curry with Carrot and Parsnip*

# Barbecued Peppered Chicken with Chilli Sauce

This is a simple dish to make and the chicken can be marinated 2 days ahead.

*2 single chicken breast fillets*
*2 cloves garlic, crushed*
*2 teaspoons grated fresh ginger*
*1/2 teaspoon cracked black peppercorns*
*2 tablespoons chopped fresh coriander*
*3 teaspoons chopped lemon grass*
*1 tablespoon light soy sauce*
*1 tablespoon oil*
CHILLI SAUCE
*1 small red chilli, finely chopped*
*1/3 cup (80ml/2¹/₂fl oz) white vinegar*
*pinch salt*
*3 teaspoons sugar*
*1 clove garlic, crushed*

Trim any fat from the chicken. Place the chicken into a non-aluminium dish. Combine the garlic, ginger, peppercorns, coriander and lemon grass in a bowl then stir in the soy sauce and oil.

Pour the marinade mixture over the chicken and turn the chicken in the dish to coat well with the marinade. Cover the dish and refrigerate for at least 3 hours or preferably overnight to allow the flavours to develop.

Make the chilli sauce by combining all the ingredients in a small saucepan then simmer, uncovered, for 3 minutes. Cool. Barbecue or grill the chicken until browned and just cooked through. Serve with the Chilli Sauce.

SERVES 2

# Chicken Livers with Chilli

Cook this dish at the last minute. The chicken livers make a delicious combination with authentic Thai flavours. Use bok choy or choy sum Chinese greens, they are available from Asian food stores and greengrocers.

*400g (12¹/₂oz) chicken livers*
*4 lemon wedges*
*1 tablespoon oil*
*1 onion, finely sliced*
*2 cloves garlic, crushed*
*1 medium red chilli, finely sliced*
*1 medium green chilli, finely sliced*
*2 tablespoons coconut milk*
*6 large Chinese greens leaves, shredded*
*3 teaspoons Thai fish sauce*
*2 tablespoons chopped fresh coriander*

Soak the chicken livers in a bowl of water with the lemon wedges for 30 minutes. Drain well and peel away any fine white membrane on the livers. Cut away any fat then halve the livers.

Heat the oil in a frying pan, add the onion and garlic, cook gently for several minutes until the onion is very soft. Add the livers and cook, turning occasionally until almost cooked through.

Add the chillies, coconut milk, Chinese greens and fish sauce. Stir gently until the Chinese greens are wilted and the livers are just cooked through (don't overcook them or they will become dry). Serve sprinkled with the coriander.

SERVES 2 TO 4

*LEFT: From top: Barbecued Peppered Chicken with Chilli Sauce; Chicken Livers with Chilli*

# Stuffed Spatchcocks with Nutty Cinnamon Rice

This very special Laotian dish would be stunning for a dinner party and is a must for an Indochinese banquet. This quantity could serve up to four people as the stuffing is quite filling. Include a soup and a salad to complete the meal.

*2 teaspoons oil*
*2 cloves garlic, crushed*
*1 onion, finely chopped*
*1 teaspoon fennel seeds*
*½ teaspoon dried chilli flakes*
*½ teaspoon ground cinnamon*
*250g (8oz) pork mince*
*2 tablespoons roasted peanuts, finely chopped*
*2 tablespoons uncooked long-grain rice*
*¾ cup (185ml/6fl oz) coconut cream*
*1 tablespoon chopped fresh mint*
*2 x 600g (19oz) spatchcocks*
*1⅔ cups (410ml/13fl oz) coconut cream, extra*
*2 cups (500ml/16fl oz) water*
*2 teaspoons fish sauce*
*1 teaspoon curry powder*
*2 sliced red chillies*
*chopped peanuts, extra*

Heat the oil in a wok or frying pan, add the garlic, onion, fennel seeds, chilli and cinnamon, stir-fry until aromatic. Add the pork mince, stir-fry until the pork has changed colour. Stir in the peanuts and rice, stir until combined. Add the coconut cream, bring to the boil, cover, reduce heat to low, cook for 10 minutes, remove the lid and stir in the mint, cool.

Spoon this stuffing mixture into the cavities of the spatchcocks, forcing any remaining stuffing under the skin around the necks. Sew the cavity openings or secure with toothpicks. Secure the legs with kitchen string and tuck the wings behind the backs.

Combine the extra coconut cream, water, fish sauce and curry powder in saucepan large enough to just fit both spatchcocks. Bring to the boil, add spatchcocks, simmer covered for about 45 minutes or until the spatchcocks are cooked through. Turn the spatchcocks once during cooking.

Remove the spatchcocks from the pan, keep warm. Return the pan to the heat, simmer the pan juices uncovered over medium heat for about 15 minutes or until thickened slightly and reduced to about 1½ cups (375ml/12fl oz) liquid – the mixture will form a light sauce. Using sharp kitchen scissors and a sharp knife, cut down the centres of the spatchcocks. Serve with the sauce, sprinkle with the sliced chillies and extra chopped peanuts if preferred.

SERVES 2 TO 4

VARIATION

If spatchcocks are unavailable, substitute with a small chicken.

*RIGHT: Stuffed Spatchcocks with Nutty Cinnamon Rice*

# Chicken with Thai Seasoning

*2 single chicken breast fillets*
*8 large English spinach leaves*
*2 teaspoons grated lime zest*
*1 tablespoon chopped fresh coriander*
*1 teaspoon sambal oelek*
*oil*
SAUCE
*2 tablespoons white vinegar*
*1 teaspoon brown sugar*
*$^{1}/_{2}$ teaspoon cornflour*
*1 tablespoon water*
*$^{1}/_{4}$ teaspoon grated lime zest*
*2 teaspoons small fresh coriander leaves*
*$^{1}/_{2}$ small red chilli, seeded and finely sliced*

Remove the tenderloin fillet from the underside of the chicken fillets. Chop the tenderloin fillets very finely, place in a bowl and reserve for the seasoning.

Cut a pocket into the side of each chicken fillet without cutting right through.

Drop the spinach into a saucepan of boiling water until just wilted. Drain and rinse under cold water then drain on paper towels. Chop the spinach and add to the chopped chicken in the bowl. Add the lime zest, coriander and sambal oelek and mix well.

Push the spinach seasoning into the pockets in the chicken fillets then toothpick or skewer the openings firmly together to seal.

Brush the fillets with oil and place on a baking tray. Bake in a 180°C (350°F) oven for about 20 minutes or until the chicken is cooked through.

While the chicken is cooking, make the sauce. Combine the vinegar, sugar and combined cornflour and water in a small saucepan. Stir over heat until the mixture boils and thickens. Add the remaining ingredients and mix well. Cut the chicken into slices and serve with the sauce and Steamed Jasmine Rice.

SERVES 2

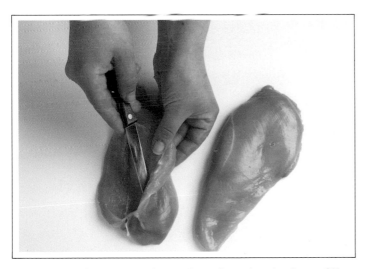

Cut a pocket into the side of each chicken fillet without cutting right through.

Toothpick or skewer the openings together.

*RIGHT: Chicken with Thai Seasoning*

# Tofu and Pork Stack with Bean Sauce

This dish looks very impressive for a dinner party and is a different way of using tofu. These stacks can be cut into halves or even quarters to serve more people.

*1 tablespoon dried shrimp*
*¹/₂ x 450g (14¹/₂oz) block firm or hard tofu*
*2 cloves garlic, crushed*
*250g (8oz) pork mince*
*3 green shallots (spring onions), finely chopped*
*2 teaspoons fish sauce*
*1 tablespoon oyster sauce*
*¹/₂ teaspoon oil or Chilli Oil (see THE ESSENTIALS)*
*coriander sprigs for garnishing*
BEAN SAUCE
*²/₃ cup (165ml/5¹/₂fl oz) water*
*2 teaspoons fish sauce*
*1 teaspoon bean sauce*
*1 tablespoon tomato paste*
*1 teaspoon sugar*
*1 teaspoon cornflour*

Cover the dried shrimp with hot water in a small bowl, stand 30 minutes, drain, chop finely. Drain the tofu well, pat dry with paper towels. Cut into 1.5cm (½in) thick slices. You will need 4 slices measuring about 10cm x 6cm (4in x 2½in), this will depend on the original size of the tofu.

Combine the garlic, pork mince, green shallots (spring onions), fish sauce and shrimp in a bowl. Spread half the pork mixture over one of the tofu slices, top with another tofu slice to form a sandwich. Repeat with the remaining pork mixture and tofu.

Place the stacks on a lightly greased baking tray, brush with combined oyster sauce and oil, bake in a 190°C (375°F) oven for about 30 minutes or until the pork mixture is cooked, brushing during cooking with any remaining oyster sauce mixture.

Make the bean sauce by combining the water, fish sauce, bean sauce, tomato paste, sugar and cornflour in a small saucepan, bring to the boil, simmer, uncovered for 1 minute. Serve the stacks with the Bean Sauce and garnish with the sprigs of coriander.

SERVES 2

VARIATION
You can substitute chicken mince for pork mince and add some finely chopped chilli to the pork mixture if you would like the dish hot and spicy

# Glazed Pork Ribs with Capsicum

*500g (16oz) American-style pork spare ribs*
*2 teaspoons oil*
*1 teaspoon shrimp paste*
*2 tablespoons sugar*
*1¹/₂ tablespoons water*
*1 onion, cut into 8 wedges*
*3 cloves garlic, sliced*
*1 small red capsicum (pepper), chopped*
*1 small green capsicum (pepper), chopped*
*75g (2¹/₂oz) sugar snap peas*
*1¹/₂ tablespoons light soy sauce*
*1 tablespoon chopped fresh coriander*

Cut the ribs into 2 rib sections. Heat the oil in a large frying pan, cook the ribs for about 30 minutes, turning during cooking, until they are browned and cooked through. Drain on paper towels.

Drain all but 1 tablespoon of fat from the pan. Add the shrimp paste, sugar and water to the pan, stir until the sugar has dissolved. Add the onion, garlic, capsicums (peppers) and sugar snap peas, cook, stirring, for about 3 minutes or until the vegetables are cooked but still crisp. Return the ribs to the pan and add the soy sauce and coriander, stir until well combined and the ribs have heated through.

SERVES 2

*RIGHT: From left: Glazed Pork Ribs with Capsicum;*
*Tofu and Pork Stack with Bean Sauce*

# Peppered Pork and Omelette Rolls

This dish can be made a day ahead and reheated in the oven before serving. Cover the dish with a lid or foil before reheating so the rolls do not become dry.

*3 eggs*
*2 tablespoons well-flavoured chicken stock*
*2 tablespoons chopped fresh coriander*
*2 tablespoons oil*
*300g (9¹/₂oz) minced pork*
*3 cloves garlic, crushed*
*2 teaspoons good quality purchased or home-made green curry paste*
*150g (5oz) green beans, chopped*
*1 teaspoon sambal oelek*
*¹/₃ cup (80ml/2¹/₂fl oz) coconut cream*
*¹/₄ cup (7g/¹/₄oz) chopped mixed fresh coriander and basil*
*6 large bok choy or choy sum leaves*
*Thai sweet chilli sauce, optional*

Beat the eggs, stock and coriander in a bowl until well combined. Heat a lightly oiled 20cm (8in) omelette pan, add enough of the egg mixture to coat the base of the pan (approximately one-sixth). Cook until the omelette is set, remove from the pan. Repeat with the remaining egg mixture to make 6 omelettes.

Heat the oil in a frying pan, add the pork, garlic, curry paste, beans and sambal oelek. Cook, stirring occasionally, until the pork is cooked and the beans are almost tender. Add the coconut cream and herbs, simmer for about 1 minute or until thick then remove from the heat.

Add the bok choy leaves to a pan of boiling water, simmer until just wilted. Drain and rinse under cold water then drain well on paper towels.

Spread a leaf over each omelette, spoon the pork mixture onto the leaves and roll up the omelettes.

Place the rolls into a greased ovenproof dish, cover with foil and bake in a 180°C (350°F) oven for about 15 minutes or until heated through. Serve the rolls with Thai sweet chilli sauce.

SERVES 2 TO 4

# Spiced Pork Curry

Massaman curry paste is available from Asian food stores. It adds a special flavour to this curry.

*2 tablespoons oil*
*375g (12oz) pork neck fillet, sliced*
*1 small onion, finely chopped*
*2 tablespoons massaman curry paste*
*2 medium potatoes, cubed*
*1¹/₂ cups (375ml/12fl oz) well-flavoured chicken stock*
*¹/₄ cup (60ml/2fl oz) coconut cream*
*2 teaspoons Thai fish sauce*
*2 tablespoons chopped roasted unsalted peanuts*
*2 tablespoons chopped coriander*

Heat the oil in a saucepan, add the pork and cook until lightly browned on both sides. Remove the pork from the pan. Add the onion to the pan, cook until soft. Add the curry paste and cook for several seconds.

Add the potatoes, stock, coconut cream, fish sauce and peanuts. Simmer uncovered for about 15 minutes or until the potato is just cooked. Add the pork to the pan and simmer a further few minutes or until the pork is almost cooked through. Stir through the coriander and serve with rice or noodles.

SERVES 2 TO 4

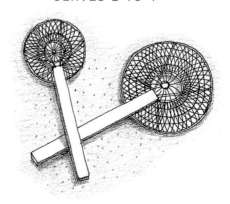

# Spicy Pork Ribs

Pork ribs are great to chew on especially when they have been marinated in a spicy mixture. Use the lean American-style ribs for best results.

*750g (1¹/₂lb) American-style pork ribs*
*(8cm (3in) in length)*
*2 tablespoons oil*
*1 tablespoon good quality purchased or*
*home-made red curry paste*
*2 tablespoons lime juice*
*1 tablespoon chopped lemon grass*
*2 teaspoons grated fresh ginger*
*2 tablespoons chopped fresh coriander*

Cut the ribs into 4 rib sections. Combine the oil, curry paste, juice, lemon grass, ginger and coriander in a bowl and mix well. Brush the rib sections thoroughly with the marinade then place in a non-aluminium dish. Cover the dish and refrigerate for at least 3 hours or preferably overnight to allow all the flavours to develop.

Place the ribs on a wire rack over a baking dish. Bake in a 200°C (400°F) oven, brushing with the marinade, for about 30 minutes or until browned and cooked through.

SERVES 2 TO 4

~ *Tip* ~

Chop several stalks of lemon grass, grate a large piece of fresh ginger and chop a good handful of fresh coriander. Combine them all together and freeze in 2 tablespoon lots to have on hand for a quick marinade addition.

# Barbecued Pork with Spinach

This dish is very simple and easy to prepare. Cook it at the last minute and serve with a noodle or rice dish. Remember to increase or decrease the sambal oelek for a hotter or milder chilli flavour.

*1 tablespoon oil*
*2 cloves garlic, finely chopped*
*200g (6¹/₂oz) piece Chinese barbecued pork, sliced*
*1 bunch English spinach, coarsely shredded*
*2 tablespoons oyster sauce*
*2 tablespoons well-flavoured chicken or*
*vegetable stock*
*2 teaspoons sambal oelek*

Heat the oil in a wok or large frying pan, add the garlic and pork, stir-fry for 2 minutes. Add the spinach, oyster sauce, stock and sambal oelek and simmer while stirring gently until the spinach is just wilted.

SERVES 2 TO 4

VARIATIONS
- Use 2 sliced single chicken breast fillets in place of the pork if preferred
- Add 60g (2oz) of peeled and deveined cooked prawns with the spinach
- Add 12 quartered stalks of fresh asparagus with the spinach

# Stir-Fried Pork with Red Curry Paste

Use a good quality red curry paste or a home-made red curry paste (see THE ESSENTIALS). You can increase the curry paste for a spicier curry if you like.

*400g (12¹/₂oz) lean diced pork*
*2 tablespoons oil*
*1 tablespoon good quality purchased or home-made red curry paste*
*2 kaffir lime leaves, finely shredded or 1 teaspoon grated lime zest*
*2 small zucchini (courgettes), finely sliced*
*1 tablespoon Thai fish sauce*
*1 tablespoon well-flavoured chicken stock*
*2 tablespoons shredded fresh basil*

Remove any fat from the pork. Heat the oil in a wok or large frying pan, add the pork and stir-fry until lightly browned.

Add the curry paste, lime leaves, zucchini (courgettes), fish sauce and stock. Stir-fry until the pork is just cooked through. Stir in the basil then serve immediately.

SERVES 2 TO 4

VARIATIONS

◆ Add a good handful of cooked cubed sweet potato to add a sweet flavour and delicious texture
◆ Use half the pork and substitute the other half with chicken thigh fillets for variety

# Pork with Citrus Marinade and Spinach

All parts of the coriander plant can be used in Thai cooking. Chop the stems with the leaves as they are full of flavour too. The roots are also used in all types of dishes such as the marinade in this recipe.

*400g (12¹/₂oz) pork neck fillet*
*2 coriander roots, finely chopped*
*1 tablespoon chopped fresh coriander leaves and stems*
*1 tablespoon chopped fresh lemon grass*
*1 tablespoon Thai sweet chilli sauce*
*1 tablespoon lime juice*
*1 tablespoon oil*
SPINACH
*1 bunch English spinach*
*1 tablespoon oil*
*1 clove garlic, crushed*
*1 tablespoon Thai sweet chilli sauce*

Remove any fat from the pork. Place the pork into a non-aluminium dish. Combine the coriander roots, leaves and stems, lemon grass, chilli sauce, lime juice and oil then pour over the pork, turning the pork to coat well in the marinade. Cover the dish and refrigerate for at least 3 hours.

Prepare the spinach by removing the stems. Heat the oil in a wok or large frying pan, add the garlic and spinach leaves, cover and cook until the spinach is wilted. Add the sauce and stir gently to combine. Keep the spinach warm while cooking the pork.

Drain the pork and grill, pan-fry or barbecue, brushing with the marinade, until just cooked through. Slice the pork and serve it on a bed of the spinach mixture.

SERVES 2 TO 4

*RIGHT: From top: Stir-Fried Pork with Red Curry Paste; Pork with Citrus Marinade and Spinach*

# Layered Pork and Mushroom Casserole

*1 tablespoon dried shrimp*
*300g (10oz) pork scotch fillet*
*2 teaspoons oil*
*1 small carrot, thinly sliced*
*3 teaspoons chopped fresh ginger*
*1 teaspoon chopped fresh coriander root*
*4 green shallots (spring onions), chopped*
*100g (3½oz) large mushrooms, sliced*
*1 potato, thinly sliced*
*1 teaspoon sesame oil*
*1 teaspoon curry powder*
*2 cloves garlic, crushed*
*1 teaspoon fish sauce*
*½ cup (125ml/4fl oz) water*
*1 tomato, cut into 10 wedges*

Cover the shrimp with hot water in a small bowl; stand for 30 minutes. Drain then chop finely.

Cut the pork into 3cm (1¼in) pieces. Heat the oil in a wok or medium frying pan until hot, add the pork, stir-fry until browned, drain on paper towels. Transfer the pork to a 4 cup (1 litre/32fl oz) capacity ovenproof casserole dish, sprinkle with the chopped shrimp. Arrange the carrot over the top of the pork.

Add the ginger and coriander root to the wok, cook for about 1 minute or until aromatic. Add the green shallots (spring onions) and mushrooms, stir-fry for about 3 minutes or until the mushrooms are lightly browned. Spoon the mushroom mixture over the carrot. Arrange the potato over the mushrooms.

Heat the sesame oil in the same wok, add the curry powder and garlic, cook for 1 minute or until aromatic. Add the fish sauce and water, bring to the boil, pour over the potatoes.

Arrange the tomato over the potatoes, cover and bake in a 180°C (350°F) oven for 1 hour. Sprinkle with coriander if preferred, serve with rice or bread.

SERVES 2 TO 4

# Ginger Pork Steaks with Honey Spiced Onions

The pork is pan-fried in this dish, but you could barbecue it instead. You may prefer to serve it as a whole steak with the honey glazed onions on the side, a great idea for a barbecue.

*1 tablespoon grated fresh ginger*
*2 cloves garlic, crushed*
*1 teaspoon freshly ground black pepper*
*1 teaspoon grated lime zest*
*2 pork loin medallions*
*1 tablespoon oil*
*¼ teaspoon five spice powder*
*pinch chilli powder*
*2 onions, each cut into 8 wedges*
*3 green shallots (spring onions), cut into*
*4cm (1½in) lengths*
*1 tablespoon honey*
*2 teaspoons fish sauce*
*2 tablespoons light soy sauce*
*1 tablespoon lime juice*

Combine the ginger, garlic, pepper and lime zest in a small bowl, rub the mixture all over the pork, cover and refrigerate for 1 hour.

Heat the oil in a frying pan, cook the pork until browned all over and just cooked through. Remove from the pan, slice into thin strips, keep warm.

Heat the same pan, add the five spice powder, chilli powder, onions, and green shallots (spring onions), stir-fry quickly until the shallots start to turn a bright green. Add the honey, fish sauce, soy sauce and lime juice, stir until combined. Serve with the sliced pork and drizzled with the pan juices.

SERVES 2

~ 88 ~

# Pork and Bean Sprout Pancakes

The rice flour gives these pancakes a very delicate crispy texture. They are best made in a well seasoned or non-stick frying pan.

2 tablespoons split yellow mung beans
1½ tablespoons rice flour
1½ tablespoons plain flour
¼ teaspoon ground turmeric
1 tablespoon chopped fresh garlic chives
½ cup (125ml/4fl oz) coconut milk
1 egg, lightly beaten
¼ cup (60ml/2fl oz) water, approximately
250g (8oz) pork neck fillet
3 cloves garlic, crushed
1 tablespoon fish sauce
¼ teaspoon freshly ground black pepper
2 tablespoons oil, approximately
1 onion, thinly sliced
75g (2½oz) mushrooms, thinly sliced
½ cup (40g/about 1½oz) bean sprouts

Place the mung beans in a small saucepan, cover with cold water, bring to the boil, simmer uncovered for about 20 minutes or until just tender, drain.

Combine the flours, turmeric and chives in a bowl. Whisk in the coconut milk, egg and enough water to form a thin batter the consistency of pouring cream. Leave to stand while preparing the pork.

Cut pork into very thin slices. Combine the pork, garlic, fish sauce and pepper in a small bowl. Heat some of the oil in an omelette pan or frying pan (preferably non-stick). Add the pork mixture and onion and stir-fry over high heat until pork changes colour and onion begins to soften. Remove from pan.

Reduce heat to medium, stir prepared batter and pour half into the pan, swirling to coat base. Sprinkle half the cooked mung beans all over the pancake. Place half the pork and onion mixture, half the mushrooms, and half the bean sprouts over half the pancake. Cover and cook over medium heat for about 5 minutes or

until well browned underneath and cooked through.

Using a spatula, carefully fold the pancake in half and slide onto a serving plate. Keep warm while preparing the second pancake in the same way.

SERVES 2

# Steamed Pork Patties with Minted Peanut Sauce

250g (8oz) pork mince
100g (3½oz) ham, finely chopped
2 cloves garlic, crushed
2 teaspoons grated fresh ginger
1 teaspoon fish sauce
1 egg white
3 green shallots (spring onions), finely chopped
2 tablespoons uncooked long-grain rice
1½ tablespoons toasted sesame seeds
sesame oil
MINTED PEANUT SAUCE
1 quantity Peanut Sauce (see THE ESSENTIALS)
1 tablespoon chopped fresh mint

Combine the pork mince, ham, garlic, ginger, fish sauce, egg white and green shallots (spring onions) in a bowl. Using lightly oiled hands, divide mixture into 4 portions and mould them into patties about 7½cm (3in) in diameter. Roll the patties in the combined rice and sesame seeds.

Lightly brush a steamer with sesame oil. Place the patties in the steamer and steam for about 20 minutes or until cooked and the rice is puffed and tender.

Make the Minted Peanut Sauce by combining the Peanut Sauce and half the mint in a small bowl, sprinkle with the remaining mint.

Serve the patties with a small bowl of the Minted Peanut Sauce for each person.

SERVES 2

# Warm Salad of Egg and Tofu

Julienne vegetables are made by cutting the vegetables into very fine sticks usually about 5cm (2in) in length.

*200g (6¹/₂oz) firm or hard tofu, cubed*
*4 green shallots (spring onions), sliced*
*1 clove garlic, crushed*
*¹/₄ teaspoon chilli powder*
*1 tablespoon light soy sauce*
*1 tablespoon lime juice*
*1 tablespoon oil*
*¹/₂ x 425g (13¹/₂oz) can mini corn, quartered lengthwise*
*1 stick celery, julienned*
*1 small red capsicum (pepper), julienned*
*2 soft to medium-boiled eggs, quartered*
*coriander leaves*

Place the tofu in a non-aluminium dish. Pour over the combined green shallots (spring onions), garlic, chilli powder, soy sauce and lime juice. Stir to coat the tofu in the marinade. Cover the dish and refrigerate for a few hours.

Drain the tofu and save the marinade. Heat the oil in a frying pan, add the tofu and cook until browned all over. Remove the tofu from the pan. Add the corn, celery and capsicum (pepper) to the pan, and cook, stirring for 2 minutes. Add the marinade and the tofu and simmer for a few seconds.

Place the vegetables in a serving dish, top with the tofu and eggs then drizzle with any liquid left in the pan. Sprinkle with the coriander leaves and serve immediately.

SERVES 2 TO 4

# Nutty Broccoli and Chilli Omelette

This omelette can be cut into cubes and served with drinks or served as a vegetarian main course.

*250g (8oz) broccoli, chopped*
*3 eggs*
*2 teaspoons light soy sauce*
*1–2 medium red chillies, chopped*
*¹/₄ cup (35g/about 1oz) finely chopped roasted cashew nuts or peanuts*
*3 tablespoons chopped fresh coriander*
*1 tablespoon oil*
*2 cloves garlic, crushed*
*6 green shallots (spring onions), finely chopped*

Cook the broccoli in a pan of boiling water until just tender; drain very well. Combine the eggs, soy sauce, chillies, cashew nuts and coriander in a bowl then add the broccoli and mix well.

Heat the oil in a 20cm (8in) omelette pan, add the garlic and green shallots (spring onions), cook gently until the green shallots are soft. Pour in the egg mixture and stir well.

Cover and cook over low heat until the base of the omelette is set and browned. Finish cooking the omelette under a hot grill until set in the centre. Cut into wedges.

SERVES 2 TO 4

VARIATIONS
- In place of broccoli, you can use either potato, kumara (red sweet potato) or pumpkin
- Any nuts can be used in place of cashew nuts or peanuts in this omelette choose from almonds, pistachios, brazil nuts or pine nuts

*LEFT: From top: Warm Salad of Egg and Tofu; Nutty Broccoli and Chilli Omelette*

# Tofu and Vegetable Fresh Spring Rolls with Spicy Dressing

The rice paper holds well in these fresh-tasting spring rolls. They can be made ahead of time, cover well with plastic wrap and refrigerate until ready to serve.

*1 bunch English spinach*
*1 carrot, julienned*
*2 green shallots (spring onions), cut into*
*8cm (3in) strips*
*10 x 18cm (7in) square rice paper sheets*
*150g (5oz) firm or hard tofu, cut into 8cm*
*(3in) thin strips*
*10 long mint leaves*
SPICY DRESSING
*2 tablespoons white vinegar*
*2 teaspoons sugar*
*1 tablespoon Thai sweet chilli sauce*
*2 tablespoons lime juice*
*1 clove garlic, crushed*
*¼ teaspoon sesame oil*
*2 teaspoons chopped fresh coriander*

Discard the spinach stems and place the leaves into a saucepan. Cover and cook the spinach gently until wilted, drain well and cool. Squeeze any excess liquid from the cooled spinach.

Drop the carrot into a saucepan of boiling water and boil until tender; drain well. Drop the green shallots (springs onions) into boiling water for 30 seconds or until softened; drain well.

Make the Spicy Dressing by combining all the ingredients in a bowl. Mix well.

Making 1 roll at a time, soak a sheet of rice paper in warm water until only just softened. Place onto a board. Top with some of the spinach, carrot, shallot, tofu and mint leaves.

Drizzle with a little dressing. Roll up firmly, folding in the sides. Repeat with the remaining rice paper, vegetables, tofu, mint and some of the dressing. Serve the spring rolls with the remaining dressing.

MAKES 10

Top the rice paper with some spinach, carrot, shallot, tofu and mint leaves.

Roll up firmly, folding in the sides.

*RIGHT: Tofu and Vegetable Fresh Spring Rolls with Spicy Dressing*

# Eggplant and Potato Curry

You can use regular or sweet potato in this curry. Other root vegetables such as swede, kumara (red sweet potato) or celeriac can be used in place of the potato.

*1 tablespoon oil*
*1 small onion, chopped*
*2 cloves garlic, crushed*
*2 tablespoons chopped lemon grass*
*1–2 medium red chillies, chopped*
*2 teaspoons grated fresh ginger*
*2 tablespoons chopped fresh coriander*
*6 long baby eggplants (aubergines), sliced*
*6 small new potatoes, halved*
*1/4 cup (30g/1oz) green peas*
*3/4 cup (185ml/6fl oz) well-flavoured vegetable stock*
*1/2 cup (125ml/4fl oz) coconut milk*

Process the oil, onion, garlic, lemon grass, chillies, ginger and coriander to a paste consistency. Place the paste into a saucepan and cook gently for several minutes.

Add the eggplants (aubergines), potatoes, peas, stock and coconut milk. Simmer covered, for about 15 minutes or until the vegetables are tender.

SERVES 2 TO 4

VARIATIONS

◆ If long baby eggplants are not available, use a chopped large eggplant
◆ For a richer creamier curry, use coconut cream in place of coconut milk

# Marinated Tofu with Vegetables

Use the firmest tofu you can find. It is generally called firm or hard tofu and is ideal for marinating and frying. The texture is quite "meaty" and provides a substantial vegetarian meal.

*250g (8oz) firm or hard tofu*
*2 cloves garlic, crushed*
*1 tablespoon light soy sauce*
*1 tablespoon oyster sauce*
*2 tablespoons oil*
*2 teaspoons sesame seeds*
*1 small onion, thinly sliced*
*60g (2oz) green beans, sliced*
*1/2 red capsicum (pepper), chopped*
*1/2 cup (15g/1/2oz) small mint leaves*

Cut the tofu into 1cm (1/2in) thick slices then place into a non-aluminium dish. Combine the garlic, sauces, half the oil and sesame seeds and pour over the tofu. Turn the tofu to coat in the marinade. Cover the dish and refrigerate for several hours to allow the flavours to develop.

Drain the tofu and save the marinade. Heat the remaining oil in a frying pan, add the tofu and cook until browned on both sides. Remove the tofu from the frying pan.

Add the onion, beans and capsicum (pepper) to the pan and stir-fry until partially cooked. Stir in the marinade and add the tofu, simmer until heated through. Add the mint leaves and serve immediately.

SERVES 2 TO 4

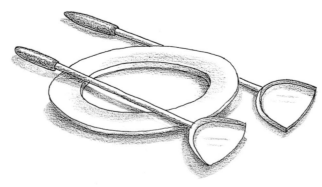

# Rice Noodle, Peanut and Spinach Stir-Fry

Use any of your favourite nuts in this stir-fry or try a mixture of nuts. For a strict vegetarian dish, you will have to use home-made red curry paste omitting the shrimp paste when making the paste.

*8 Chinese dried mushrooms*
*200g (6$^1$/$_2$oz) dried rice stick noodles*
*1 bunch English spinach*
*2 tablespoons oil*
*3–4 teaspoons good quality purchased or home-made red curry paste*
*1 clove garlic, crushed*
*$^1$/$_4$ cup (60ml/2fl oz) well-flavoured vegetable stock*
*$^1$/$_4$ cup (35g/about 1oz) finely chopped roasted peanuts*
*$^1$/$_2$ teaspoon sesame oil*

Place the mushrooms into a bowl with hot water, soak for 20 minutes. Drain and squeeze away any excess liquid. Cut the mushrooms into thin slices, discarding the tough stems.

Place the noodles into a heatproof bowl, pour over boiling water to cover. Stand the noodles for 10 minutes. Drain the noodles, tossing through a little oil to stop them from sticking together.

Halve the spinach leaves and discard the stems. Heat the oil in a wok or large frying pan. Add the curry paste and garlic, cook gently for a few seconds. Add the mushrooms, spinach and stock, stir gently until the spinach is just wilted. Add the noodles, peanuts and sesame oil and toss gently until heated through.

SERVES 2 TO 4

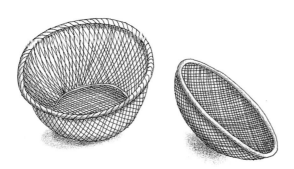

# Chick Peas and Couscous with Herbs and Coconut Cream

Couscous is a type of fine pasta made from semolina and does not need cooking, just soak in a boiling liquid.

*$^1$/$_2$ cup (90g/3oz) couscous*
*$^1$/$_2$ cup (125ml/4fl oz) well-flavoured vegetable stock*
*1 tablespoon oil*
*2 cloves garlic, crushed*
*6 green shallots (spring onions), chopped*
*2 teaspoons good quality purchased or home-made red curry paste*
*310g (10oz) can chick peas, drained*
*2 tablespoons chopped fresh coriander*
*1 tablespoon chopped lemon grass*
*$^1$/$_3$ cup (80ml/2$^1$/$_2$fl oz) coconut cream*

Place the couscous in a heatproof bowl. Bring the stock to a boil in a saucepan, pour over the couscous and mix well. Stand the couscous for 10 minutes or until the stock is completely absorbed.

Heat the oil in a wok or large frying pan, add the garlic, green shallots (spring onions) and curry paste and cook gently for 1 minute. Add the chick peas, coriander, lemon grass and coconut cream and stir until heated through. Add the couscous and toss gently with a fork until combined. Serve warm or cold.

SERVES 2 TO 4

VARIATION

100g (3$^1$/$_2$oz) dried rice stick noodles can be used in place of the couscous if preferred. Prepare the noodles as in Rice Noodle, Peanut and Spinach Stir-Fry (at left) and use the stock as part of the soaking liquid.

# Cinnamon Sausage Baguette

1 French bread stick (baguette), halved
1 quantity Peanut Sauce (see THE ESSENTIALS)
1/2 teaspoon sesame oil
1 tablespoon toasted sesame seeds
1 quantity Pickled Carrot or Cucumber (see SALADS AND VEGETABLES)
assorted lettuces such as coral, butter or cos lettuce
1 cup (80g/2½oz) bean sprouts
1/4 cup (7g/¼oz) fresh mint leaves
2 tablespoons fresh coriander leaves

CINNAMON SAUSAGE
1 tablespoon dried shrimp
1/4 cup (35g/about 1oz) couscous
1/4 cup (60ml/2fl oz) boiling well-flavoured chicken stock or water
200g (6½oz) pork mince
1 tablespoon fish sauce
4 cloves garlic, crushed
1/2 teaspoon freshly ground black pepper
6 green shallots (spring onions), finely chopped
1 teaspoon ground cinnamon
1 tablespoon sesame seeds, toasted

Split each half of French stick (baguette) lengthwise without cutting right through. Combine the Peanut Sauce with the sesame oil and sesame seeds in a small bowl. Spread some Peanut Sauce mixture onto each side of the split French stick.

To make the cinnamon sausage, cover the shrimp with hot water in a small bowl, stand for 30 minutes. Drain and chop finely. Combine the couscous and stock in a small bowl, stand for 5 minutes until all the liquid has been absorbed.

Process the shrimp, pork mince, fish sauce, garlic, pepper, green shallots (spring onions) and cinnamon until fine and smooth. Stir in the couscous. With lightly wet hands, mould mixture into a sausage shape about 5cm (2in) in diameter. Roll in sesame seeds until completely coated. Place sausage onto a 33cm (13in) square piece of baking paper or lightly greased greaseproof paper, roll up tightly and twist the ends.

Place the sausage into a steamer and steam for 20 minutes. Stand 5 minutes before unwrapping. Allow to cool slightly before slicing.

Place sliced cinnamon sausage, pickled carrot or cucumber, lettuce leaves, bean sprouts, mint and coriander leaves into the split French stick and spoon more Peanut Sauce mixture over before serving.

The sausage can also be eaten cold or sliced and barbecued, and eaten with a dipping sauce.

SERVES 4

# Crisp Tofu in Tomato Sauce

200g (6½oz) firm tofu
1 tablespoon oil
4 green shallots (spring onions), chopped
3 cloves garlic, crushed
3 ripe tomatoes, chopped
1 teaspoon fish sauce
1 tablespoon lime juice
1/4 cup (60ml/2fl oz) water
2 teaspoons tomato paste
2 tablespoons chopped fresh coriander

Drain the tofu well, pat dry with paper towels. Cut the tofu into 3cm (1¼in) pieces. Brush all over with some of the oil, place on a baking tray, grill only until lightly browned, turn pieces to brown other side.

Heat the remaining oil in a wok or saucepan, add the green shallots (spring onions) and garlic, stir over medium heat until the shallots are soft. Add the tomatoes and cook, stirring for about 3 minutes or until the tomatoes are soft. Add the fish sauce, lime juice and combined water and tomato paste, bring to the boil, then simmer uncovered for 2 minutes. Add the tofu to the wok with the coriander, stir until heated through. Serve with a bowl of steamed rice.

SERVES 2 TO 4

*LEFT: Crisp Tofu in Tomato Sauce*

# Grilled Fish Cutlets with Thai Pesto

The pesto can be made a week ahead or it can be frozen for several weeks. Pesto is an Italian word meaning ground or crushed. This is a Thai-flavoured variation of the famous Italian pesto sauce. This quantity of pesto will make 4 servings.

1 clove garlic, crushed
1 tablespoon oil
2–4 white fish cutlets
THAI PESTO
90g (3oz) bunch fresh coriander
1/2 cup (15g/1/2oz) basil leaves
2 tablespoons chopped lemon grass
2 cloves garlic, crushed
2 teaspoons Thai fish sauce
1 tablespoon lime juice
1/4 cup (60ml/2fl oz) oil
1 tablespoon Thai sweet chilli sauce

Make the pesto by roughly chopping the coriander leaves, stems and roots. Process the coriander, basil, lemon grass, garlic, fish sauce and lime juice until finely chopped. Add the oil and chilli sauce while the motor is running. Process until a paste consistency.

Combine the garlic and oil with 2 tablespoons of the Thai Pesto. Grill the fish, brushing with the garlic, oil and pesto mixture, until cooked through. Serve the fish topped with a good dollop of the remaining Thai Pesto. Place any remaining pesto into a clean jar, top with a layer of oil and refrigerate – it will keep for up to 1 week.

SERVES 2 TO 4

# Baked Whole Fish

I generally use snapper in this recipe, but any white fish can be used.

2 x 400g (12 1/2oz) whole fish, gutted and scaled
2.5cm (1in) piece fresh ginger, finely shredded
2 cloves garlic, thinly sliced
1/4 red capsicum (pepper), thinly sliced
1 medium red chilli, thinly sliced
1 1/2 tablespoons white vinegar
1 teaspoon sugar
1 tablespoon oil
coriander leaves
CHILLI SAUCE
1–2 medium red chillies
2 cloves garlic, finely chopped
3 teaspoons sugar
2 tablespoons lime juice
2 teaspoons finely chopped roasted cashew nuts

Make deep cuts, about 2cm (3/4in) apart, along both sides of the fish. Place in an ovenproof dish. Combine the ginger, garlic, capsicum (pepper), chilli, vinegar, sugar and oil in a bowl. Spoon the mixture inside the fish and over the top. Sprinkle with coriander leaves.

Cover the dish and bake in a 180°C (350°F) oven for about 20 minutes or until the fish flakes easily with a fork.

While the fish is cooking, make the chilli sauce by combining all the ingredients in a bowl and mixing well. Serve the fish with the Chilli Sauce.

SERVES 2 TO 4

*LEFT: Grilled Fish Cutlets with Thai Pesto*

# Curried Prawns with Cucumber and Asparagus

This is a very quick curry that is best made close to serving time. If you have time, make the curry paste an hour ahead. Combine the prawns with about 1 tablespoon of the curry paste; cover and refrigerate for 1 hour.

1 clove garlic, crushed
1 small onion, grated
1 tablespoon chopped lemon grass
$1/2$ teaspoon ground turmeric
1 teaspoon paprika
pinch allspice
1 teaspoon chilli powder
$1/4$ teaspoon ground cinnamon
1 teaspoon ground coriander
pinch saffron powder
2 teaspoons brown sugar
1 tablespoon lime juice
1 small green cucumber
12 spears fresh asparagus
12 medium uncooked prawns
1 tablespoon oil
$1/2$ cup (125ml/4fl oz) coconut cream
$2/3$ cup (165ml/5$1/2$fl oz) water
2 teaspoons fish sauce
1 teaspoon cornflour
fresh sprigs of coriander

Make a curry paste by using a mortar and pestle or a blender to blend the garlic, onion, lemon grass, turmeric, paprika, allspice, chilli powder, cinnamon, coriander, saffron, sugar and lime juice to a paste.

Halve the unpeeled cucumber lengthwise then using a teaspoon, scrape out the seeds. Cut the cucumber into 5mm ($1/4$in) slices and the asparagus into 3cm (1$1/4$in) lengths. Peel and devein the prawns, leaving the tails intact.

Heat the oil in a wok or medium saucepan, add the curry paste, cook stirring for about 2 minutes or until bubbling and the mixture is aromatic. Add the prawns, stir until well coated. Add the cucumber and asparagus, then the coconut cream and combined water, fish sauce and cornflour, bring to the boil, stirring. Simmer uncovered for 3 minutes or until the prawns are cooked and the sauce is thickened.

Serve the curry garnished with sprigs of fresh coriander and a bowl of steamed rice or crusty bread.

SERVES 2

# Grilled Crab and Prawn Cakes

A healthy alternative to the traditionally deep-fried seafood cakes, these can be eaten hot or cold. You may like to serve them as appetisers – cut into quarters.

100g (3$1/2$oz) crab meat
4 cloves garlic, crushed
4 green shallots (spring onions), finely chopped
1 tablespoon chopped fresh dill
$1/2$ teaspoon freshly ground black pepper
2 anchovy fillets, finely chopped
400g (13oz) medium uncooked prawns, peeled and deveined
1 tablespoon oil or Shallot Oil (see THE ESSENTIALS)
1 quantity Fish Dipping Sauce (see THE ESSENTIALS)
1 tablespoon tamarind purée

Process the crab meat, garlic, green shallots (spring onions), dill, pepper and anchovy fillets until very finely chopped. Add the prawns, process until mixture forms a thick paste. Divide evenly into 6 portions.

With lightly oiled hands, mould each portion of mixture into a 6cm (2$1/2$in) patty. Place the patties onto a lightly oiled griller tray, brush with oil then grill for about 5 minutes on both sides or until browned and cooked through. Serve the cakes with the Fish Dipping Sauce combined with the tamarind purée.

SERVES 2

*RIGHT: Curried Prawns with Cucumber and Asparagus*

Wooden spoon from Corso de Fiori; wood spice box from Orson & Blake

# Prawns with Lemon Grass and Chilli

Fresh kaffir lime leaves are available from Asian food stores. If you prefer, you can used dried kaffir lime leaves. Soak them in hot water for several hours before shredding them. The lime leaves add a lovely subtle lime flavour to this dish.

*500g (16oz) large uncooked prawns*
*1 tablespoon oil*
*1 teaspoon good quality purchased or home-made green curry paste*
*2 tablespoons thinly sliced lemon grass*
*1–2 medium red chillies, chopped*
*3 teaspoons Thai fish sauce*
*3 kaffir lime leaves, shredded or 1 teaspoon grated lime zest*
*1 teaspoon sugar*
*2 tablespoons coconut milk*

Peel and devein the prawns, leaving the tails intact. Heat the oil in a wok or large frying pan, add the curry paste and cook for a few seconds.

Add the prawns, lemon grass, chillies, fish sauce, lime leaves, sugar and coconut milk. Simmer gently, while stirring occasionally, until the prawns are just cooked through.

SERVES 2 TO 4

VARIATIONS

◆ Replace half the prawns with 250g of cubed firm white fish fillets
◆ Add 150g (5oz) snow peas (mangetout) with the prawns

# Char-Grilled Octopus

The marinade in this recipe can also be used with prawns, fish cubes and squid. It is best to allow the octopus to marinate overnight as this not only increases the flavour but also tenderises the octopus deliciously.

*500g (16oz) baby octopus*
*1 tablespoon light soy sauce*
*1 tablespoon oil*
*1 tablespoon dry sherry*
*2 cloves garlic, crushed*
*1 teaspoon grated lime zest*
*2 tablespoons lime juice*
*2 medium red chillies, chopped*
*2 tablespoons chopped fresh coriander*

Prepare the octopus by cutting away the heads from just below the eyes. Cut the octopus in half. Remove the black "beak" which is found in the centre of the body where all the legs meet.

Combine the soy sauce, oil, sherry, garlic, lime zest and juice, chillies and coriander in a bowl. Add the octopus and mix thoroughly. Cover and refrigerate for several hours or preferably overnight to allow the flavours to develop.

Drain the octopus and cook in a char-grill pan or on a barbecue grill until just cooked through. If you like, you can bring any remaining marinade to a boil in a saucepan and serve with the octopus as a sauce.

SERVES 2 TO 4

*RIGHT: From top: Prawns with Lemon Grass and Chilli; Char-Grilled Octopus*

# Seafood with Herbs, Chilli and Garlic

*1 small uncooked crab*
*6 medium uncooked prawns*
*6 small black mussels*
*2 tablespoons oil*
*200g (6¹/₂oz) firm white fish fillet, cut into*
*2.5cm (1in) cubes*
*3 small cleaned squid, sliced into rings*
*1 tablespoon good quality purchased or home-made red curry paste*
*2 fresh coriander roots, finely chopped*
*2 cloves garlic, finely chopped*
*1 tablespoon chopped lemon grass*
*1–2 small red chillies, thinly sliced*
*2 tablespoons Thai fish sauce*
*1 tablespoon oyster sauce*
*¹/₂ cup (125ml/4fl oz) water*
*1 cup (30g/1oz) chopped mixed basil, coriander and mint*
*4 green shallots (spring onions), cut into short lengths*

Prepare the crab by sliding a strong knife under the top body shell from the back, lever off the shell. Scrape away the white gills along the sides. Wash well. Using a sharp knife, cut the body into quarters. Remove the large claws and crack with a nut cracker along the length (or tap gently along the claws with meat mallet).

Peel and devein the prawns leaving the tails intact. Scrub the mussels and pull away the fibrous "beards" – you may have to scrape away any seaweed on the shells.

Heat half the oil in a large wok or frying pan, add enough fish cubes to cover the base and cook through. Place the fish in a bowl and set aside. Repeat with the remaining fish. Add the squid rings to the wok, stir-fry for about 1 minute or until they are just cooked. Add to the fish. You may need to clean the wok.

Heat the remaining oil in the wok, add the curry paste, coriander roots, garlic, lemon grass and half the chillies. Cook 1 minute, stir in the sauces and water.

Add the crab, prawns and mussels to the wok, making sure the thick pieces of crab and the mussels are on the base and submerged in the liquid. Cover the wok and simmer for about 5 minutes or until the mussels open and the crab is cooked through. Gently stir in the fish cubes, squid, herbs and green shallots (spring onions), toss gently until heated through. Sprinkle with the remaining chillies before serving.

SERVES 2 TO 4

# Baked Noodles with Prawns and Broccoli

*100g (3¹/₂oz) dried rice stick noodles*
*1 tablespoon oil*
*1 small onion, thinly sliced*
*2 cloves garlic, crushed*
*12 uncooked king prawns, peeled and deveined*
*2 teaspoons grated fresh ginger*
*1 tablespoon chopped lemon grass*
*1 medium red chilli, finely chopped*
*2 tablespoons chopped fresh coriander*
*2 teaspoons oyster sauce*
*2 teaspoons light soy sauce*
*¹/₄ teaspoon sesame oil*
*100g (3¹/₂oz) broccoli, cut into small florets*
*2 tablespoons well-flavoured chicken stock*

Place the noodles in a heatproof bowl and cover with boiling water. Stand for 5 minutes then drain well.

Heat the oil in a saucepan, add the onion and garlic and cook gently until the onion is very soft and lightly browned. Remove from the heat and stir in the noodles and all the remaining ingredients. Mix very well.

Spoon the mixture into 2 x 2 cup (500ml/16fl oz) capacity ovenproof dishes. Cover and bake in a 180°C (350°F) oven for about 25 minutes or until the prawns are cooked through. Serve in the dishes.

SERVES 2

*RIGHT: Seafood with Herbs, Chilli and Garlic*

# Lamb Rolls with Sesame Peanut Sauce

These rolls also look attractive served as an entrée for 4 people. They can be made
several hours ahead and kept covered in the refrigerator.

3cm (1¼in) piece fresh ginger

½ large avocado, sliced

2 tablespoons lime juice

1 tablespoon oil

330g (10½oz) lamb fillets

1 tablespoon dry sherry

1 tablespoon fish sauce

150g (5oz) daikon radish, julienned

75g (2½oz) thinly sliced ham, julienned

1 small carrot, julienned

⅓ cup (10g/⅓oz) fresh mint leaves

4 x 22cm (8½in) round sheets rice paper (banh
trang)

SESAME PEANUT SAUCE

1 quantity Peanut Sauce (see THE ESSENTIALS)

1 tablespoon sesame seeds, toasted

½ teaspoon sesame oil

Cut the ginger into thin strips. Combine the avocado
and lime juice in a bowl. Heat the oil in a frying pan,
add the lamb, cook turning until well browned and
just cooked, this will take about 8 minutes. Add the
sherry and fish sauce, allow the mixture to bubble,
remove from the heat then cool. Cut the lamb into 8
long strips, drizzle with the pan juices.

Have the fillings prepared in order of use to help
with the quick wrapping of the rolls. First the avocado
mixture, then the lamb, radish, ham, carrot, ginger and
mint leaves.

Soak a sheet of rice paper in a bowl of warm water
until soft and pliable. Place onto a board. Place a
quarter of the avocado slices, 2 lamb strips, a quarter of
the radish, ham strips, carrot strips, ginger and mint
leaves along the centre of the rice paper. Roll the rice
paper up quickly and tightly to enclose the filling.
Repeat with remaining sheets of rice paper and fillings.

Make the Sesame Peanut Sauce by combining the
Peanut Sauce with half the seeds and the sesame oil in
a small bowl. Divide the sauce between individual
bowls, sprinkle with the remaining sesame seeds.

Serve the rolls whole or cut diagonally into halves
with Sesame Peanut Sauce for each person.

SERVES 2

Place the fillings onto the softened rice paper.

Roll the rice paper up quickly and tightly.

LEFT: Lamb Rolls with Sesame Peanut Sauce

# Fish Strips and Prawns with Ginger and Herbs

Choose a firm fish fillet that will hold together when cooked. If you really enjoy the flavour of ginger, add twice the amount for extra flavour.

*300g (9$^1$/$_2$oz) boneless white fish fillet, cut into*
*5cm (2in) strips*
*6 uncooked king prawns, peeled and deveined*
*2 tablespoons lime juice*
*2 teaspoons grated fresh ginger*
*2 coriander roots, finely chopped*
*2 tablespoons chopped fresh coriander leaves*
*1 tablespoon chopped fresh basil leaves*
*2 teaspoons Thai fish sauce*
*1 tablespoon oil*

Place the fish and prawns in a non-aluminium dish. Add the combined lime juice, ginger, coriander roots and leaves, basil, fish sauce and oil then mix thoroughly.

Cover the dish and refrigerate for at least 2 hours to allow the flavours to develop. Add the fish mixture to a wok or large frying pan, simmer, while stirring occasionally, for about 5 minutes or until the fish and prawns are just cooked through. Serve with steamed rice or noodles.

SERVES 2 TO 4

# Creamy Beef Curry

I use rump steak in this recipe, but you can use any tender cut of beef such as boneless sirloin, eye fillet or rib-eye fillet.

*300g (9$^1$/$_2$oz) tender cut of beef*
*1 tablespoon oil*
*1 tablespoon good quality purchased or home-made green curry paste*
*1 cup (250ml/8fl oz) coconut milk*
*2 teaspoons Thai fish sauce*
*1 teaspoon sugar*
*$^1$/$_2$ x 425g (14oz) can mini corn pieces*
*$^1$/$_3$ cup (60g/2oz) canned straw mushrooms, drained*
*$^1$/$_2$ cup (15g/$^1$/$_2$oz) small basil leaves*

Cut the beef into thin slices, discarding any fat. Heat the oil in a wok or large frying pan, add the beef and stir-fry over high heat until browned. Remove the beef from the wok.

Add the curry paste to the wok and cook gently for a few seconds. Add the coconut milk, fish sauce, sugar, corn and mushrooms. Bring to a boil then simmer for 5 minutes. Add the beef and basil and simmer about 2 minutes or until the beef is heated through. Serve with steamed rice.

SERVES 2 TO 4

### ~ Tip ~

To cut meat into thin slices, wrap it in plastic or freezer wrap in a single layer then partially freeze. Remove the meat from the wrap and cut into thin slices while it is partially frozen using a sharp knife.

# Roast Lamb with Thai Seasoning

Ask the butcher to bone the leg of lamb for you.

*1.5kg (3lb) leg of lamb, boned*
*³/₄ cup (150g/5oz) Steamed Jasmine Rice*
*2 tablespoons chopped lemon grass*
*3 teaspoons good quality purchased or home-made*
*red curry paste*
*6 green shallots (spring onions), finely chopped*
*6 kaffir lime leaves, shredded or 2 teaspoons*
*grated lime zest*
*¹/₄ cup (7g/¹/₄oz) shredded mixed fresh basil and*
*coriander leaves*
*1 egg*
*1 teaspoon oyster sauce*
*oil*

Trim any excess fat from the lamb. Cut almost through the thicker part of the lamb, lay it open and overlap the edge with the rest of the lamb to create a large flat piece. Combine the rice, lemon grass, curry paste, green shallots (spring onions), lime leaves, herbs, egg and oyster sauce in a bowl and mix well.

Spoon the mixture along the centre of the lamb. Roll the lamb up firmly, holding it together with skewers. Tie the lamb with kitchen string at 2cm (³/₄in) intervals to keep it securely rolled. Place the lamb on a wire rack over a baking dish; brush with oil. Bake in a 180°C (350°F) oven for about 1 hour or until cooked as desired – test this by piercing the lamb with a skewer in the thickest part. If the juices are a little pink, the lamb is medium cooked. Cover the lamb with foil and stand for 10 minutes before slicing. Serve the lamb with Chilli Lime Sauce (see THE ESSENTIALS).

SERVES 4 TO 6

# Thai-Style Minced Beef

Use this mixture to fill pancakes or toasted jaffles or toss through cooked noodles.

*300g (9¹/₂oz) lean minced beef*
*2 tablespoons chopped lemon grass*
*1 small onion, finely chopped*
*2 cloves garlic, crushed*
*1–2 medium red chillies, finely chopped*
*1 tablespoon oil*
*2 tablespoons well-flavoured beef stock*
*1 tablespoon oyster sauce*
*3 teaspoons light soy sauce*
*2 tablespoons coconut cream*
*1 teaspoon sugar*
*¹/₄ cup (7g/¹/₄oz) chopped fresh coriander*
*lettuce leaves*

Combine the beef, lemon grass, onion, garlic and chillies in a bowl. Refrigerate for at least 3 hours to allow the flavours to develop.

Heat the oil in a wok or frying pan, add the beef mixture and stir-fry until all the beef is coloured and there are no large lumps. Add the stock, sauces, coconut cream and sugar and simmer until thick. Stir in the coriander and serve the mixture in lettuce leaves.

SERVES 2 TO 4

VARIATIONS

◆ In place of the minced beef, use chopped or sliced boneless sirloin steak. Then serve the dish with steamed rice or noodles

◆ Drop 6 large leaves of silverbeet (Swiss chard) in a pan of boiling water until just wilted. Drain well. Spoon the beef mixture onto the leaves, fold in the sides of the leaves and roll up firmly. Serve with bottled Thai sweet chilli sauce

# Slow-Cooked Spicy Beef

Any cut of beef that requires long slow cooking can be used in this recipe. The slow cooking brings out the delicious beef flavour and makes the beef melt-in-the-mouth tender.

*400g (12¹/₂oz) beef chuck steak*
*2 tablespoons oil*
*1–2 tablespoons Penang curry paste*
*1 small onion, chopped*
*2 cloves garlic, crushed*
*1 cup (250ml/8fl oz) well-flavoured beef stock*
*¹/₄ cup (60ml/2fl oz) coconut cream*
*2 tablespoons chopped fresh coriander*

Remove any excess fat from the beef then cut the beef into 3cm (1¹/₄in) pieces. Heat the oil in a medium saucepan, add the beef and cook until browned all over. Remove from the saucepan.

Add the curry paste, onion and garlic to the saucepan, cook gently until the onion is soft. Add the beef and stock, cover and simmer, partially covered, for 1 hour. Stir in the coconut cream and simmer for a further 30 minutes or until the beef is tender and the sauce is thick. Stir in the coriander, mix thoroughly and serve immediately.

SERVES 2 TO 4

# Lamb with Eggplant and Tamarind

Tamarind concentrate is available from Asian food stores. It is a very thick, almost black, liquid made from tamarind pods. Tamarind adds a refreshing fruity and sour flavour to dishes such as this one.

*400g (12¹/₂oz) lamb backstrap or boneless lamb*
*¹/₄ cup (60ml/2fl oz) oil*
*1 small onion, finely chopped*
*1 clove garlic, crushed*
*1 small eggplant (aubergine), cubed*
*1 teaspoon tamarind concentrate*
*3 teaspoons Thai fish sauce*
*³/₄ cup (185ml/6fl oz) well-flavoured chicken stock*
*2 tablespoons coconut milk*
*1–2 medium red chillies, chopped*
*2 tablespoons shredded fresh basil*

Trim any fat from the lamb, cut the lamb into 1cm (¹/₂in) thick slices. Heat half the oil in a wok or large frying pan, add the lamb and stir-fry until browned all over, remove from the wok.

Heat the remaining oil in the wok, add the onion, garlic, eggplant and tamarind concentrate. Stir-fry until the onion is soft then stir in the fish sauce, stock, coconut milk and chillies. Simmer, covered, for about 15 minutes or until the eggplant is soft. Add the lamb and simmer until just cooked through. Sprinkle with the basil and serve immediately.

SERVES 2 TO 4

### ~ Tip ~

The safest way to chop chillies is by wearing rubber gloves. Or, if you have only 1 or 2 to chop, hold the chilli by the stalk and chop using a pair of kitchen scissors. The hottest part of a chilli is its seeds. If you want to reduce the spiciness, remove the seeds.

*LEFT: From top: Lamb with Eggplant and Tamarind; Slow-Cooked Spicy Beef*

# Char-Grilled Lamb and Eggplant with Ginger Sauce

A wonderfully easy dish to prepare, it can be made several hours ahead and eaten cold.

6 lamb cutlets
3 cloves garlic, crushed
1/4 teaspoon freshly ground black pepper
2 long baby eggplants (aubergines)
oil
1 tablespoon chopped fresh coriander
GINGER SAUCE
1 quantity Fish Dipping Sauce (see THE ESSENTIALS)
1 teaspoon grated fresh ginger
1 tablespoon bean sauce

Combine the cutlets with the garlic and pepper in a medium bowl, cover and refrigerate for 1 hour. Halve the eggplants (aubergines) lengthwise.

Barbecue or grill the cutlets and the eggplants on a well oiled hotplate until browned and just cooked.

Make the Ginger Sauce by combining the Fish Dipping Sauce with the ginger and bean sauce in a small jug or bowl.

Arrange the lamb cutlets and eggplants on a serving plate, drizzle with the Ginger Sauce and garnish with the coriander.

SERVES 2

# Beef Steaks with Slivered Mango and Vegetables

This recipe makes quite a hearty quantity of vegetables and is a delicious sauce to be served over barbecued meat. Substitute beef round or beef fillet if you prefer.

2 tablespoons oil
2 New York cut beef steaks
1 small red capsicum (pepper)
1 small green capsicum (pepper)
1 small carrot
2 spring (bulb) onions
1 tablespoon oil, extra
2 tablespoons light soy sauce
1 tablespoon rice vinegar
1 tablespoon fish sauce
1 teaspoon cornflour
1/4 cup (60ml/2fl oz) water
1/4 teaspoon hot chilli sauce
1/4 cup (7g/1/4oz) fresh mint leaves
1 medium mango, sliced
sprigs of fresh coriander

Heat the oil in a frying pan, cook the steaks until well browned on both sides and cooked as desired. Drain on paper towels and keep hot.

While the steaks are cooking, prepare the vegetables. Cut the capsicums (peppers) and carrot into long thin strips. Quarter the spring (bulb) onions lengthwise, including some of the green tops.

Heat the extra oil in the same pan, add the capsicums, carrot and spring onions, stir-fry for about 3 minutes or until lightly browned. Add the soy sauce, vinegar, fish sauce and cornflour blended with the water and chilli sauce, bring to the boil. Add the mint and mango, remove from the heat, stir well.

Cut the steaks into thin strips or leave whole. Serve the mango and vegetable mixture with the steaks, drizzle with the pan juices and sprinkle with coriander.

SERVES 2

*RIGHT: From top: Char-Grilled Lamb and Eggplant with Ginger Sauce; Beef Steaks with Slivered Mango and Vegetables*

# Beef in Peanut Sauce

Penang curry paste is available from Asian food stores. You will usually find it in a small can. I use what I need from the can and spoon the rest into a clean jar to keep in the refrigerator for up to 2 months (it is usually used by then).

*1½ tablespoons Penang curry paste*
*4 kaffir lime leaves or 1–2 teaspoons grated lime zest*
*½ cup (125ml/4fl oz) well-flavoured beef or chicken stock*
*¾ cup (185ml/6fl oz) coconut milk*
*400g (12½oz) beef rump steak or boneless sirloin steak, thinly sliced*
*1 tablespoon Thai fish sauce*
*⅓ cup (50g/1½ oz) ground roasted peanuts*
*1 medium red chilli, sliced*
*½ cup (15g/½oz) mixed basil and coriander leaves*
*1 green shallot (spring onion), chopped*

Combine the curry paste, lime leaves, stock and coconut milk in a pan. Bring to a boil and boil for 1 minute. Add the beef, fish sauce, peanuts and chilli. Simmer about 10 minutes or until the beef is just cooked. Stir in the herbs and green shallot (spring onion) and serve immediately.

SERVES 2 TO 4

VARIATIONS

◆ You could use lamb or chicken in this recipe in place of the beef
◆ Add a handful of green peas to the sauce with the beef

# Lamb's Liver with Garlic and Black Pepper

This dish can also be made with chicken livers or calve's liver. Make sure you remove the thin membrane from around the liver as this can make it a little chewy. Don't overcook the liver.

*400g (12½oz) lamb's liver*
*2 tablespoons lemon juice*
*2 tablespoons oil*
*4 cloves garlic, finely chopped*
*4 coriander roots, finely chopped*
*1 teaspoon coarsely ground black peppercorns*
*3 teaspoons Thai fish sauce*
*2 tablespoons chopped fresh coriander leaves*
*1 tablespoon lime juice*

Soak the liver in a bowl of cold water with the lemon juice for 30 minutes. Drain and peel away the thin membrane from the outside of the liver.

Cut the liver into 1.5cm (about ½in) thick slices. Heat the oil in a large frying pan, add the liver slices and cook over a high heat until browned on both sides and just cooked through. Remove from the pan.

Add the garlic, coriander roots and peppercorns to the pan and cook gently for a few seconds. Stir in the fish sauce, coriander leaves and lime juice then add the liver, simmer until heated through then serve immediately.

SERVES 2 TO 4

*RIGHT: Lamb's Liver with Garlic and Black Pepper*

# Salads and Vegetables

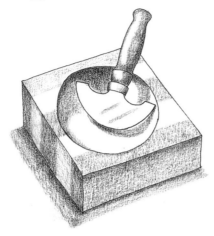

R aw salads and vegetable dishes form the basis of any Vietnamese, Laotian and Cambodian meal. The pickled vegetables can be decoratively cut and arranged to accompany a rice or seafood dish.

The flavours and ingredients of Thailand add so much interest and a myriad of textures to vegetable and salad dishes. Some of the salads make perfect luncheon dishes that are light and nutritious and the vegetable dishes work well with soups and curries. All the dishes use ingredients that are readily available and you will find them simple to prepare.

*RIGHT: Spicy Eggplant and Shredded Chicken*

# Greens with Chilli and Herbs

This dish can be made with any of the green leafy vegetables. I have used chicory which is very nutritious and combines well with the Vietnamese flavourings.

*500g (16oz) chicory*
*2 tablespoons oil*
*4 cloves garlic, finely chopped*
*2 small red chillies, finely chopped*
*2 tablespoons shredded fresh mint*
*1 tablespoon fresh coriander leaves*
*1½ tablespoons vegetable stock*
*3 teaspoons fish sauce*

Trim the stalks from the chicory, wash the stalks and leaves thoroughly then drain well. Cut the stalks into finger length pieces.

Half fill a large saucepan with water, bring to the boil. Add the chicory stalks then add the leaves 1 minute later. Boil gently for about 3 minutes after adding the leaves or until the stalks and leaves are tender. Drain.

Heat the oil in the pan, add the garlic and chillies, cook until aromatic then add the herbs, stock and fish sauce, simmer 1 minute.

Return the chicory to the pan and toss well until heated through before serving.

SERVES 2 TO 4

# Spicy Eggplant with Shredded Chicken

The flavours of barbecued eggplant (aubergine), pepper and chicken with lots of fresh herbs make this dish delicious and very nutritious with only a minimal amount of oil used. If made up to 3 hours ahead, this dish tastes even better because the flavours have time to develop.

*2 long baby eggplants (aubergines)*
*1 single chicken breast fillet*
*1 small long green 'banana' pepper, quartered*
*1 small tomato, sliced*
*2 cloves garlic, sliced*
*2 teaspoons chopped fresh mint*
*1 tablespoon chopped fresh coriander*
*1 small red chilli, finely chopped*
**DRESSING**
*2 tablespoons fish sauce*
*1½ tablespoons rice vinegar*
*½ teaspoon sesame oil*

Cut the eggplants (aubergines) lengthwise into 5mm (¼in) thick slices. Barbecue or grill the chicken until cooked, cool slightly then cut into thin shreds.

Barbecue or grill the eggplants and pepper until lightly browned. The skin of the pepper will bubble and burn. Place the pepper in a paper bag or cover to help the skin steam and peel away easier. Remove the skin and slice the pepper into thin strips.

Combine the chicken, eggplants, pepper, tomato, garlic, mint, coriander and chilli in a bowl.

Make the dressing by combining the fish sauce, vinegar and sesame oil in a jar, shake well. Pour the dressing over the chicken and vegetables. Serve warm or refrigerate 1 hour before serving.

SERVES 2

# Pickled Vegetables with Bacon

If you haven't the time to make the pickled carrot and cucumber, you will find a variety of pickled vegetables at any Asian grocery store that will work just as well in this recipe; you will need about 350g (11oz) of vegetables. If you can't find fresh mini corn, use half a can of mini corn.

*1 tablespoon oil*
*3 cloves garlic, sliced*
*3cm (1¼in) piece fresh ginger, peeled and finely sliced*
*3 bacon rashers, chopped*
*75g (2½oz) fresh mini corn, halved lengthwise*
*75g (2½oz) snow peas (mangetout)*
*3 green shallots (spring onions), sliced*
*1 quantity Pickled Carrot (see recipe at right), drained*
*1 quantity Pickled Cucumber (see recipe at right), drained*
*230g (7oz) can sliced bamboo shoots, drained*
*1 tablespoon rice vinegar*
*1 tablespoon fish sauce*
*1 tablespoon bean sauce*
*2 teaspoons lime juice*

Heat the oil in a wok or frying pan, add the garlic, ginger and bacon, stir-fry for 2 minutes. Add the corn and stir-fry for 3 minutes. Add the snow peas (mangetout), green shallots (spring onions), pickled carrot and pickled cucumber, stir-fry for 2 minutes.

Add the bamboo shoots, vinegar, fish sauce, bean sauce and lime juice then stir until heated through.

SERVES 2

VARIATION

In place of the bacon you can use Chinese barbecued pork

# Pickled Carrot, Daikon Radish or Cucumber

This is a very easy way of pickling vegetables and because they are not actually boiled, I find them nice and crisp, with plenty of flavour. They are a classic accompaniment for many Vietnamese meals, can be made ahead and are perfect if you are entertaining.

*2 small carrots, 150g (5oz) daikon radish or*
*2 small green cucumbers*
*½ cup (125ml/4fl oz) rice vinegar*
*2 teaspoons sugar*
*¼ teaspoon salt*
*½ cup (125ml/4fl oz) boiling water*

Peel the carrots or daikon radish, cut into 3mm (⅛in) thick slices. If using cucumbers, do not peel, but cut them into slices as for the carrots.

Combine the vinegar, sugar, salt and boiling water in a bowl, stir until the sugar and salt have dissolved. Cool to room temperature. Add the vegetables to the vinegar mixture, stand for at least 2 hours before using.

Store in a jar in the refrigerator and ensure the vegetables are fully covered by the vinegar mixture to prevent any mould from forming. Pickled vegetables will keep refrigerated for up to 2 weeks.

MAKES ABOUT 1 MEDIUM JAR

# Lamb Patty Salad

This salad can be served while the lamb patties are still warm or when they are cold. It makes a lovely summer main course salad.

400g (12¹/₂oz) lean minced lamb
1 tablespoon grated fresh ginger
1 teaspoon grated lime zest
2 cloves garlic, crushed
6 green shallots (spring onions), finely chopped
1 egg
1 teaspoon sambal oelek
1 tablespoon oil
1 bunch rocket (arugula)
100g (3¹/₂oz) snow peas (mangetout)
1 small red capsicum (pepper), thinly sliced
DRESSING
2 tablespoons oil
1 tablespoon lime juice
1 clove garlic, crushed
salt and ground black pepper

Combine the lamb, ginger, lime zest, garlic, green shallots (spring onions), egg and sambal oelek in a bowl and mix thoroughly.

Shape tablespoons of the mixture into patties. Heat the oil in a large frying pan, add the lamb patties and cook until they are browned on both sides and just cooked through. Drain the patties on paper towels.

Tear the rocket (arugula) into large pieces. Add the snow peas (mangetout) to a medium pan of boiling water and boil 1 minute. Drain the snow peas and rinse under cold water then drain thoroughly. Make the dressing by combining all the ingredients in a lidded jar, shake well.

Arrange the lamb patties, rocket, snow peas and capsicum (pepper) on serving plates then drizzle with the dressing.

SERVES 2 AS A MAIN COURSE
OR 4 AS AN ENTREE

Shape tablespoons of mixture into patties.

Drain the patties on paper towels.

*RIGHT: Lamb Patty Salad*

# Glazed Pumpkin and Zucchini

Another easy yet flavoursome way with vegetables, this dish is best served with meat dishes such as the Grilled Lemon Grass and Chilli Chicken, the Grilled Crab and Prawn Cakes or the Dry Beef and Sweet Potato Curry. I have chosen to leave the skin on the pumpkin as it looks more attractive, and the skin is edible if the pumpkin is very young.

*350g (11oz) nugget pumpkin*
*2 medium zucchini (courgettes)*
*1 tablespoon oil*
*2 cloves garlic, halved*
*3cm (1¼in) piece fresh ginger, peeled and finely shredded*
*2 teaspoons fish sauce*
*1 tablespoon honey*
*¼ cup (60ml/2fl oz) well-flavoured vegetable or chicken stock*
*2 teaspoons sesame seeds, toasted*

Cut the unpeeled pumpkin into wedges about 2cm (¾in) thick. Halve the zucchini (courgettes) lengthwise then cut each half into thirds.

Heat the oil in a wok or large frying pan, add the zucchini (courgettes), cook over high heat until browned all over, drain on paper towels. Add the pumpkin, brown on both sides, then add the garlic and ginger, stir-fry for about 1 minute or until aromatic.

Add the fish sauce, honey and stock, bring to the boil, cover and simmer for 3 minutes, return the zucchini to the pan, simmer, covered for a further 2 minutes or until the vegetables are tender. Serve sprinkled with the sesame seeds.

SERVES 2

# Grapefruit, Sprout and Cucumber Salad

A beautifully crisp, light and healthy salad that is a delicious meal in itself or a perfect salad accompaniment for a banquet meal. I've used the delicately flavoured pink grapefruit for its pretty colour, but it is not always readily available, so yellow grapefruit can be used.

*1 small pink or yellow grapefruit*
*1 small green cucumber*
*150g (5oz) cooked chicken, shredded*
*4 medium cooked prawns, peeled, deveined and halved*
*1 small carrot, grated*
*1 cup (80g/2½oz) bean sprouts*
*1 cup (80g/2½oz) snow pea (mangetout) sprouts*
*1 tablespoon fresh mint leaves*
*1 tablespoon fresh coriander leaves*
*1 tablespoon unsalted roasted cashew nuts*
*1 quantity Fish Dipping Sauce (see THE ESSENTIALS)*

Peel and segment the grapefruit. Halve the cucumber lengthwise then using a teaspoon, scoop out the seeds and cut the cucumber into slices.

Combine the grapefruit, cucumber, chicken, prawns, carrot, sprouts and herbs in a bowl. Sprinkle with the cashew nuts, cover and refrigerate for up to 2 hours. Before serving, drizzle with Fish Dipping Sauce.

SERVES 2 TO 4

VARIATION
Substitute any cooked meat instead of the chicken and prawns or grill a single chicken breast fillet until just cooked then cool and slice it

*RIGHT: From top: Glazed Pumpkin and Zucchini; Grapefruit, Sprout and Cucumber Salad*

# Vegetable Salad with Chilli Lime Dressing

This salad can be made a day ahead. Combine with the dressing before serving.

*1 carrot*
*100g (3¹/₂oz) green beans*
*150g (5oz) broccoli*
*1 red capsicum (pepper)*
*6 green shallots (spring onions), chopped*
*2 tablespoons chopped fresh mint*
*2 tablespoons chopped fresh coriander*
CHILLI LIME DRESSING
*¹/₂ teaspoon grated lime zest*
*1¹/₂ tablespoons lime juice*
*1 teaspoon light soy sauce*
*1 tablespoon Thai sweet chilli sauce*
*1 tablespoon oil*

Cut the carrot into thin sticks. Cut the beans into 5cm (2in) lengths. Cut the broccoli into small florets. Cut the capsicum (pepper) into 5cm (2in) strips. Cook the carrot, beans and broccoli separately in a saucepan of boiling water until almost tender, rinse under cold water and drain well.

Make the Chilli Lime Dressing by combining all the ingredients in a lidded jar, shake well.

Combine the cooked vegetables with the capsicum, green shallots (spring onions), mint, coriander and the dressing in a serving bowl then toss well.

SERVES 4

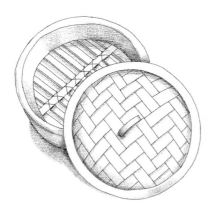

# Chicken, Scallop and Orange Salad

Prawns can be used in place of the scallops in this fresh-flavoured salad. If you are preparing the salad ahead, prepare the avocado and add to the salad at the last minute.

*2 single chicken breast fillets*
*100g (3¹/₂oz) scallops*
*green tops of 6 green shallots (spring onions), sliced*
*1 orange, segmented*
*100g (3¹/₂oz) canned bamboo shoot, julienned*
*1 avocado, sliced*
DRESSING
*2 tablespoons oil*
*2 tablespoons orange juice*
*1 teaspoon grated lime zest*
*2 tablespoons chopped fresh coriander*
*1 teaspoon Thai fish sauce*

Place the chicken in a small frying pan, cover with water or chicken stock. Cover and simmer for about 10 minutes or until just cooked through, remove from the pan and cool. Add the scallops to the liquid in the frying pan and simmer for about 2 minutes or until just cooked. Drain the scallops and cool.

Make the dressing by combining all the ingredients in a lidded jar, shake well. Cut the chicken into slices. Combine the chicken, scallops, green shallot tops (spring onion), orange segments, bamboo shoot and avocado in a bowl. Add the dressing and toss gently. Serve immediately.

SERVES 2 TO 4

VARIATION

You can use half a purchased barbecued chicken and cooked prawns in place of the chicken fillets and the scallops. Cut the chicken meat into slices, discarding the skin and fat. Peel and devein the prawns

# Thai Beef Salad

This salad is a traditional Thai salad. The ingredients combine to give a refreshingly spicy flavour. You can make the beef mixture a day ahead if you like – this allows the flavours to develop.

*375g (12oz) piece boneless sirloin steak*
*4 green shallots (spring onions), sliced*
*1 tablespoon shredded fresh mint*
*1 tablespoon fresh coriander leaves*
*2 tablespoons lime juice*
*1 tablespoon oil*
*2 teaspoons Thai fish sauce*
*1 teaspoon light soy sauce*
*1 clove garlic, crushed*
*1 small red chilli, finely chopped*
*mignonette lettuce leaves*

Trim any fat from the steak. Grill or pan-fry the steak until medium rare, remove and cool.

Cut the steak into thin strips then combine with the green shallots (spring onions), mint, coriander, lime juice, oil, fish sauce, soy sauce, garlic and chilli in a bowl. Spoon the mixture onto the lettuce then serve immediately.

SERVES 2 TO 4

VARIATION

Lamb leg steaks or pork butterfly steaks can be used in place of the beef

# Fish Salad with Mint and Beans

Choose a firm fish fillet that will hold together when cooked. If you cannot find snake beans (yard long beans), substitute with green beans.

*1 tablespoon oil*
*200g (6¹/₂oz) boneless white fish fillet, thinly sliced*
*100g (3¹/₂oz) snake beans (yard long beans), cut into 2.5cm (1in) lengths*
*80g (2¹/₂oz) small snow peas (mangetout)*
*¹/₂ small green coral lettuce*
*¹/₂ cup (15g/¹/₂oz) small fresh mint leaves*
DRESSING
*2 tablespoons oil*
*2 green shallots (spring onions), finely chopped*
*2 tablespoons lime juice*
*2 teaspoons Thai fish sauce*
*¹/₂ teaspoon sugar*
*¹/₄ teaspoon chilli powder*

Heat the oil in a wok or large frying pan, add the fish a handful at a time and cook, turning gently and without breaking until cooked through. Remove from the wok and allow to cool.

Add the snake beans (yard long beans) and snow peas (mangetout) to a medium pan of boiling water, boil about 1 minute then drain and rinse well under cold water before draining thoroughly. Make the dressing by combining all the ingredients in a lidded jar, shake well.

Combine the beans, snow peas, torn lettuce leaves, mint and the dressing in a serving bowl. Add the fish and toss gently to combine.

SERVES 2 TO 4

# Eggplant Salad

This salad makes an excellent accompaniment for a barbecue. If long baby eggplants are not available, use small regular eggplants and cut them into smaller pieces once they are cooked.

*8 long baby eggplants (aubergines)*
*oil*
*2 teaspoons Thai fish sauce*
*2 teaspoons light soy sauce*
*1/2 teaspoon sesame oil*
*1 clove garlic, crushed*
*1/2 teaspoon brown sugar*
*2 green shallots (spring onions), finely chopped*
*1 tablespoon chopped fresh basil or mint*
*1/2–1 teaspoon sambal oelek*

Cut the eggplants (aubergines) diagonally into 1cm (1/2in) thick slices. Brush with oil and grill until browned and soft, allow to cool.

Toss the eggplants with the combined fish sauce, soy sauce, sesame oil, garlic, brown sugar, green shallots (spring onions), basil and sambal oelek in a bowl and mix thoroughly. Stand 1 hour before serving.

SERVES 4

# Vegetable Stir-Fry

Any Chinese greens can be used in this stir-fry.

*1 tablespoon oil*
*2 cloves garlic, crushed*
*12 spears fresh asparagus, quartered*
*1 red capsicum (pepper), thinly sliced*
*125g (4oz) broccoli, cut into small florets*
*1 bunch choy sum or other Chinese greens*
*6 green shallots (spring onions), chopped*
*1 tablespoon Thai fish sauce*
*1 tablespoon sambal oelek*
*4 kaffir lime leaves, shredded or 1–2 teaspoons grated lime zest*

Heat the oil in a wok or large frying pan, add the garlic, asparagus, capsicum (pepper) and broccoli and stir-fry until almost tender. Add the shredded choy sum, green shallots (spring onions), fish sauce, sambal oelek and lime leaves. Stir-fry until the choy sum is wilted and the vegetables are still a little crunchy.

SERVES 2 TO 4

# Greens and Reds in Spicy Sauce

Bok choy is available from Asian food stores and greengrocers.

*10 fresh asparagus spears, cut into 2.5cm (1in) lengths*
*100g (3 1/2oz) green beans, cut into 2.5cm (1in) lengths*
*1 small radicchio lettuce*
*1 small bunch short-stemmed bok choy or other Chinese greens*
*2 tablespoons oil*
*2 cloves garlic, crushed*
*2 tablespoons chopped lemon grass*
*2 teaspoons grated fresh ginger*
*1 teaspoon ground cumin*
*1 tablespoon Thai fish sauce*
*1 tablespoon Thai sweet chilli sauce*
*2 tablespoons chopped fresh coriander*

Add the asparagus and beans to a pan of boiling water and boil for about 1 minute or until just tender. Drain well. Tear the radicchio leaves into halves. Cut the stalks from the bok choy then cut the leaves in half.

Heat the oil in a wok or large frying pan, add the garlic, lemon grass, ginger and cumin and cook gently for several seconds. Add the asparagus, beans and the bok choy stalks, stir-fry for 1 minute. Add the bok choy leaves and radicchio with all the remaining ingredients. Stir-fry until the leaves are barely wilted then serve immediately.

SERVES 2 TO 4

# Barbecued Duck Salad

You can buy Chinese barbecued duck from Chinese barbecued food stores. They are usually quite happy to sell a half duck. If you prefer, you can use a barbecued chicken.

*¹⁄₂ Chinese barbecued duck*
*8 large cos lettuce leaves, coarsely shredded*
*¹⁄₄ cup fresh coriander leaves*
DRESSING
*2 tablespoons oil*
*2 tablespoons lime juice*
*¹⁄₄ teaspoon sesame oil*
*2 teaspoons Thai fish sauce*
*¹⁄₄ teaspoon chilli powder*
*4 green shallots (spring onions), finely chopped*
*¹⁄₂ teaspoon sugar*

Remove all the meat and skin from the duck bones. Remove the skin and all the fat from the duck meat. Slice the duck meat thinly. Slice any lean crispy skin thinly and discard any fatty skin. Combine the duck meat and skin with the lettuce and coriander in a bowl.

Make the dressing by combining all the ingredients in a lidded jar, shake well. Pour the dressing over the duck mixture and toss well before serving.

SERVES 2 TO 4

VARIATION
English spinach or mignonette lettuce can be used in place of the cos lettuce

# Noodle and Bean Salad

Broad beans are much more attractive with their outer skins removed. If you are pressed for time ignore this step. Serving this salad is made simpler if you cut the noodles into 5cm (2in) lengths.

*100g (3¹⁄₂oz) frozen or fresh shelled broad beans*
*200g (6¹⁄₂oz) green beans, cut into 2.5cm (1in) lengths*
*¹⁄₂ x 375g (12oz) packet thin fresh egg noodles, cut into shorter lengths*
DRESSING
*¹⁄₄ cup (60ml/2fl oz) oil*
*2 tablespoons lime juice*
*1 clove garlic, crushed*
*1 teaspoon Thai fish sauce*
*2 green shallots (spring onions), finely chopped*
*2 tablespoons chopped fresh coriander*

Add the broad beans to a large saucepan of boiling water, boil for about 5 minutes or until tender. Remove the beans using a slotted spoon and rinse under cold water then drain well.

Add the green beans and the noodles to the saucepan, boil for 2 minutes, drain and rinse under cold water then drain thoroughly.

Make the dressing by combining all the ingredients in a lidded jar, shake well. Remove the outer skins from the broad beans. Combine all the beans, noodles and the dressing in a bowl and toss well to combine.

SERVES 2 TO 4

# Green Pawpaw, Pork and Carrot Salad

Green pawpaw (papaya) may be available at your local greengrocer or at an Asian food store which sells fresh produce. If it is unavailable, substitute green mango or turnip. The pork can be cooked a day ahead.

*1 tablespoon dried shrimp*
*100g (3½oz) pork fillet*
*1 tablespoon finely chopped lemon grass*
*1 small fresh chilli, seeded and finely chopped*
*1 teaspoon honey*
*½ teaspoon fish sauce*
*1 teaspoon light soy sauce*
*½ small (about 75g/2½oz) green unripe pawpaw (papaya)*
*1 small carrot*
*1 small green cucumber*
*1 tablespoon shredded fresh mint leaves*
*1 tablespoon shredded fresh coriander leaves*
**DRESSING**
*1 quantity Fish Dipping Sauce (see THE ESSENTIALS)*
*1–2 teaspoons hot chilli sauce*

Cover the shrimp with hot water in a bowl, stand for 30 minutes, drain then chop finely. Cut the pork into 3mm (⅛in) thick slices.

Using a mortar and pestle or a blender, blend the lemon grass, chilli, honey, fish sauce and soy sauce until a paste consistency. Combine the pork with the chilli mixture in a small bowl, mix well. Cover, refrigerate at least 1 hour or overnight.

Place the pork slices in a single layer on a wire rack over a baking tray, bake in a 180°C (350°F) oven for about 20 minutes or until just cooked, cool. Cut into thin strips.

Using a sharp knife, cut the pawpaw (papaya), carrot and cucumber into long and very thin strips; this way they will stay crisper, otherwise coarsely grate them lengthwise.

Combine the shrimp, pork, pawpaw, carrot, cucumber, mint and coriander in a serving bowl.

Make the dressing by combining the Fish Dipping Sauce and the chilli sauce in jar, shake well. Pour the dressing over the salad and serve.

SERVES 2 TO 4

Place the pork slices on a wire rack over a baking tray.

Cut the pawpaw, carrot and cucumber into thin strips.

*RIGHT: Green Pawpaw, Pork and Carrot Salad*

# Vegetable Platter with a Dipping Sauce

A vegetable platter is a must for any Vietnamese banquet, especially with such dishes as the Oven-Baked Marinated Pork Fillet or the Steamed Whole Fish with Lemon Grass and Chilli. Use any variety of lettuces, vegetables or sprouts that are in season.

*1 small green cucumber*
*1/2 bunch fresh asparagus spears, trimmed*
*1/2 cup (20g/about 1/2oz) alfalfa and onion sprouts*
*1 small tomato, cut into 8 wedges*
*1/4 cup (7g/1/4oz) fresh mint leaves*
*1/4 cup (7g/1/4oz) fresh coriander leaves*
*1 carambola (star fruit), sliced*
*assorted lettuce leaves such as red coral, radicchio*
*or cos*
*1 quantity Fish Dipping Sauce or Peanut Sauce,*
*(see THE ESSENTIALS)*

Slice the cucumber lengthwise into thin strips. Add the asparagus to a saucepan of boiling water, boil until just tender. Drain and rinse under cold water, drain well.

Arrange the cucumber, asparagus, sprouts, tomato, herbs, carambola (star fruit) and lettuces on a serving platter. Each person takes a lettuce leaf, fills it with some vegetables and herbs and perhaps some meat such as the Marinated Pork Fillet, forms a parcel and dips it in a sauce before eating.

SERVES 2 TO 4 PEOPLE

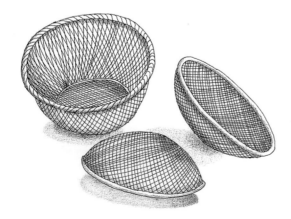

# Chicken and Basil Salad

This lovely salad is perfect for a summer lunch, and can be prepared ahead to be served cold. Just keep the cooked chicken mixture separate until you are ready to serve.

*2 sticks celery*
*1 small carrot*
*2 green shallots (spring onions)*
*6 leaves red coral lettuce*
*1 small red onion, thinly sliced*
*1 tablespoon oil*
*3 cloves garlic, sliced*
*1 single chicken breast fillet, thinly sliced*
*2 tablespoons fresh basil leaves*
*2 tablespoons fresh mint leaves*
*2 tablespoons fish sauce*
*1/3 cup (80ml/2 1/2fl oz) lime juice*
*1 tablespoon rice vinegar*
*2 teaspoons sweet chilli sauce*

Cut the celery, carrot and green shallots (spring onions) into thin strips about 6cm (2 1/2in) long.

Arrange the lettuce leaves on serving plates. Combine the celery, carrot, green shallots and onion in a bowl, pile into the lettuce leaves.

Heat the oil in a frying pan, add the garlic, stir for about 1 minute or until aromatic. Add the chicken, stir-fry for 2 minutes, then stir in the herbs, stir-fry until the herbs have wilted and the chicken is cooked. Remove from the heat, add the fish sauce, lime juice, vinegar and sweet chilli sauce, stir until well combined. Spoon the chicken mixture over the vegetables then drizzle with the pan juices.

SERVES 2

VARIATION
200g (6 1/2oz) of pork or beef can be used in place of the chicken

# Green Beans with Cauliflower and Scallops

Buy the scallops with the orange roe (coral) attached as these present beautifully with their creamy white and orange colours with the vegetables.

*100g (3½oz) scallops with roe attached*
*2 teaspoons fish sauce*
*2 cloves garlic, crushed*
*¼ teaspoon freshly ground black pepper*
*1 onion*
*100g (3½oz) green beans*
*250g (8oz) cauliflower*
*1 tablespoon oil*
*1 tablespoon chopped lemon grass*
*1 tablespoon grated fresh ginger*
*2 teaspoons light soy sauce*
*½ cup (125ml/4fl oz) well-flavoured fish stock or water*
*1 tablespoon lime juice*

Combine the scallops, fish sauce, garlic and pepper in a small bowl, cover and refrigerate for 1 hour.

Cut the onion into thin wedges. Cut the beans into 5cm (2in) lengths. Cut the cauliflower into florets.

Heat the oil in a wok or frying pan, add the onion, lemon grass, and ginger, stir-fry for 1 minute, add the cauliflower, soy sauce and stock, bring to the boil, reduce heat and simmer covered for 3 minutes. Add the scallop mixture and beans, simmer covered for a further 2 minutes or until scallops are just cooked. Stir in the lime juice then serve.

SERVES 2

VARIATION

Fresh uncooked prawns may be substituted for the scallops in this recipe if preferred

# Lamb, Lime and Watercress Salad

Prepare the salad up to 2 hours ahead and drizzle with dressing just before serving.

*200g (6½oz) lamb fillet*
*2 cloves garlic, crushed*
*1 tablespoon lime juice*
*2 teaspoons peanut butter*
*pinch chilli powder*
*2 teaspoons oil*
*3 cups (150g/5oz) fresh watercress*
*1 small red onion, sliced into rings*
*30g (1oz) sugar snap peas, halved*
*1 small red capsicum (pepper), finely chopped*
*2 teaspoons finely chopped roasted peanuts*
DRESSING
*3 teaspoons sweet chilli sauce*
*2 teaspoons fish sauce*
*¼ cup (60ml/2fl oz) lime juice*
*1 tablespoon oil*
*2 teaspoon grated fresh ginger*
*1 tablespoon water*

Cut the lamb into thin strips. Combine the lamb, garlic, lime juice, peanut butter and chilli powder in a small bowl, cover and refrigerate for 1 hour.

Heat the oil in a wok or frying pan until very hot, add the lamb and stir-fry quickly until just cooked; drain on paper towels and cool.

Make the dressing by combining all the dressing ingredients in a jar, shake well.

Combine the watercress, onion, sugar snap peas, capsicum (pepper) and lamb in large bowl, drizzle with the dressing and sprinkle with the peanuts.

SERVES 2 TO 4

VARIATION

You can substitute beef fillet or chicken breast fillet for the lamb

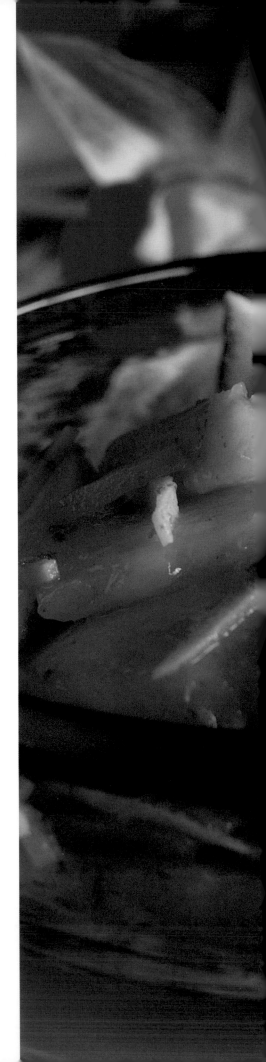

# Desserts

Thais are fond of their desserts but they are usually served at more formal dinners. An every day meal would not normally include a dessert, but a dessert type snack would often be purchased from a street vendor during the day – deep-fried bananas being a favourite along with sticky rice desserts.

The Vietnamese, Laotians and Cambodians do not have desserts often although they do eat lovely baked sweets and pastries that have a strong French influence.

The desserts in this section can be served as part of an Asian meal, as a dessert for a dinner party or served with coffee. They are mostly simple and as with many Asian desserts, use fruit and coconut as the base ingredients.

*RIGHT: Coconut Ice Cream and*
*Mango with Lime and Ginger*

# Kumara Coconut Puddings

These puddings are very simple to make and can be eaten hot or at room temperature. It is best not to boil the kumara as it can become a little too wet – steaming produces a better texture.

*280g (9oz) kumara (red sweet potato), chopped*
*1 cup (250ml/8fl oz) coconut milk*
*$^1/_3$ cup (60g/2oz) brown sugar*
*2 eggs*
*flaked almonds*

Steam or microwave the kumara (red sweet potato) until cooked. Allow to cool. Blend the kumara, coconut milk, sugar and eggs in a blender until well combined and smooth.

Pour the mixture into 4 x $^1/_2$ cup (125ml/4fl oz) capacity ovenproof dishes. Sprinkle the tops with the almonds and bake in a 180°C (350°F) oven for about 20 minutes or until the centres of the puddings are set. Serve with a slice of mango or with strawberries.

SERVES 4

VARIATIONS

◆ Add 3 tablespoons of sultanas to the mixture
◆ Add 1 teaspoon of grated fresh ginger and 2 tablespoons finely chopped glacé ginger to the mixture
◆ Add 1 teaspoon grated lime zest and 1 teaspoon grated orange zest to the mixture

# Coconut Ice Cream and Mango with Lime and Ginger

You can either scoop this ice cream or, turn it out of the pan and cut it into thick slices. It is usually best to make the ice cream a day ahead. It can also be made in an ice cream machine.

*1 cup (250ml/8fl oz) coconut milk*
*$^3/_4$ cup (185ml/6fl oz) cream*
*$^1/_4$ cup (75g/2$^1/_2$oz) caster sugar*
*2 tablespoons coconut, toasted*
*2 eggs*
*1 mango, sliced*
*2.5cm (1in) piece fresh ginger, julienned*
*1 tablespoon caster sugar, extra*
*1 teaspoon grated lime zest*
*2 tablespoons lime juice*

Heat the coconut milk, cream, sugar and coconut in a saucepan until boiling. Place the eggs into a heatproof bowl, whisk until combined. Pour the boiling coconut milk mixture over the eggs whisking all the time. Cool.

Pour the mixture into a small loaf pan, cover then freeze until firm. Chop the ice cream then beat in a bowl with an electric mixer or in a food processor until smooth. Spoon the mixture back into the pan (line the pan with foil if you wish to turn out the ice cream for serving). Cover and freeze until firm. This will take several hours.

Combine the mango, ginger, extra sugar, lime zest and juice in a bowl. Cover and refrigerate the mango mixture for several hours to allow the flavours to combine. Serve the ice cream in slices or scoops with the mango mixture.

SERVES 4

# Crisp Bananas with Caramel Sauce

I don't usually like to deep-fry foods, but this is an exception. The bananas are lovely and crisp on the outside and go beautifully with the rich caramel sauce.

*3 bananas*
*2 tablespoons grated palm sugar or brown sugar*
*2 tablespoons coconut, toasted*
*$^{1}/_{2}$ cup (75g/2$^{1}/_{2}$oz) rice flour*
*1 tablespoon sesame seeds*
*2 tablespoons caster sugar*
*$^{1}/_{4}$ cup (60ml/2fl oz) water*
*oil for deep-frying*
CARAMEL SAUCE
*2 tablespoons grated palm sugar or brown sugar*
*150g (5oz) can coconut cream*
*$^{1}/_{2}$ teaspoon rice flour or cornflour*
*2 teaspoons water*

Make the caramel sauce first. Gently heat the sugar in a small saucepan until melted. Add the coconut cream and stir until the sugar is dissolved. Stir in the combined rice flour and water and stir until the sauce boils. Keep warm while cooking the bananas.

Cut the bananas into quarters. Roll the banana pieces in the combined palm sugar and coconut, pressing the mixture on firmly.

Combine the rice flour, sesame seeds and sugar in a bowl. Gradually whisk in the water, whisking to a batter. Dip the pieces of banana into the batter and then deep-fry in hot oil until lightly browned on the outside. Drain well on paper towels.

Serve the crisp hot banana pieces with the warm caramel sauce.

SERVES 4

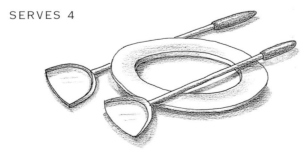

# Citrus and Ginger Fruit

This fruit salad is simple to make and is always so popular. The citrus flavours really add a zing and it is refreshing to eat on a hot summers day. This fruit could also be served with the Coconut Ice Cream.

*1 mango*
*$^{1}/_{2}$ small pineapple, chopped*
*2 kiwi fruit, chopped*
*1 banana, chopped*
*pulp of 3 passionfruit*
*2 teaspoons grated lime zest*
*1 teaspoon grated lemon zest*
*2 tablespoons lime juice*
*1 tablespoon lemon juice*
*1 tablespoon caster sugar*
*2.5cm piece fresh ginger, finely shredded*
*1 tablespoon liqueur such as Grand Marnier*
*or Malibu*

Combine the fruit in a bowl and mix well. Combine the zests, juices and sugar in a small saucepan. Stir over very low heat until the sugar is dissolved. Stir in the ginger and liqueur. Pour the mixture over the fruit and mix well. Stand for 2 hours before serving to allow the flavours to develop.

SERVES 4

VARIATIONS

◆ Use fresh strawberries and raspberries when they are at their best in summer in place of the pineapple
◆ Toss through a handful of halved coconut macaroon biscuits just before serving
◆ Add 3 tablespoons shredded fresh mint to the fruit

# Sticky Rice Dessert with Ginger Syrup

Sticky or glutinous rice is very popular with the Vietnamese and is often made into a dessert. I've used nashi pear – chop the pear just before serving.

*½ cup (125g/4oz) glutinous rice*
*¾ cup (185ml/6fl oz) water*
*3 tablespoons dried split yellow mung beans*
*2 teaspoons caster sugar*
*1 tablespoon coconut cream*
*¼ cup (45g/1½oz) brown sugar*
*3 teaspoons water, extra*
*2cm (¾in) piece fresh ginger, peeled and thinly sliced*
*1 small nashi pear, chopped*
*½ cup (125ml/4fl oz) coconut cream, extra*

Place the rice in a small bowl with enough cold water to cover. Stand overnight then drain, rinse and drain well. Bring the measured water to the boil in a medium heavy-based saucepan, add the rice and mung beans, bring back to the boil, boil for 1 minute. Place the lid on the saucepan, pour off as much water as possible, return pan to heat on lowest setting. Cook covered for 20 minutes, remove from the heat, stand for 10 minutes before removing lid. Add the caster sugar and coconut cream and toss with a fork.

While the rice is cooking, prepare the ginger syrup. Combine the brown sugar and extra water in a small saucepan, stir over low heat until the sugar has dissolved. Add the ginger and simmer uncovered for about 2 minutes or until the syrup is thick.

Using a large ice cream scoop or a spoon, scoop a quarter of the rice mixture onto dessert plates. Sprinkle nashi pear around the rice, drizzle with ginger syrup, arranging some sliced ginger on the rice.

Serve the dessert warm with a small jug of extra coconut cream for guests to drizzle over their rice.

SERVES 4

# Tropical Fruit Moulds with Mango Cream

These refreshing desserts make a cool finish to a spicy hot meal. Make them up to 2 days ahead, keeping them in the refrigerator.

*1¾ cups (435ml/14fl oz) water*
*⅔ cup (165g/5½oz) caster sugar*
*⅓ cup (80ml/2½fl oz) lime juice*
*¼ cup (60ml/2fl oz) boiling water*
*1½ tablespoons gelatine*
*565g (18oz) can jackfruit in syrup, drained and chopped*
*500 (16oz) fresh red pawpaw (papaya), chopped*
*1 kiwi fruit, peeled and sliced*
MANGO CREAM
*1 small mango, peeled and chopped*
*½ cup (125ml/4fl oz) sour cream*
*½ cup (125ml/4fl oz) coconut cream*
*2 teaspoons caster sugar*

Combine the water, sugar and lime juice in a medium saucepan. Stir over low heat until the sugar is dissolved, remove from heat.

Combine the boiling water and gelatine in a small bowl, stir until dissolved. Pour into the lime syrup, stir well then cool to room temperature.

Lightly oil 6 x 1 cup (250ml/8fl oz) capacity moulds. Pour 1 tablespoon of the lime syrup mixture into each mould, refrigerate until set. Top with about 1 tablespoon of combined jackfruit and pawpaw (papaya), pour over enough syrup to just cover the fruit, refrigerate until set. Continue layering with remaining fruit and syrup until they are all used.

While the moulds are setting, prepare the mango cream. Mash or process the mango until smooth. Combine with the sour cream, coconut cream and sugar in a small bowl.

Turn the moulds out onto dessert plates, serve with the mango cream and sliced kiwi fruit.

SERVES 6

*LEFT: Tropical Fruit Moulds with Mango Cream*

# Coconut and Sultana Rolls

These rolls are best eaten hot out of the oven, but are just as good eaten cold. They can be made up to a day ahead.

1 x 7g (¼oz) sachet dry yeast
2 tablespoons caster sugar
¾ cup (185ml/6fl oz) warm milk
2 cups (300g/9½oz) plain flour
30g (1oz) unsalted butter, chopped
½ cup (90g/3oz) chopped sultanas
1 egg yolk, lightly beaten
1 tablespoon shredded coconut for sprinkling
FILLING
1 cup (90g/3oz) coconut
1 egg white
2 tablespoons caster sugar
60g (2oz) unsalted butter, softened
1½ tablespoons grated lime zest
GLAZE
3 teaspoons caster sugar
3 teaspoons boiling water
1 teaspoon lime juice

Lightly grease a baking tray. Combine the yeast, sugar and milk in a small bowl. Cover and stand in a warm place for about 10 minutes or until frothy.

Sift the flour into a large bowl, rub in the butter then mix in the sultanas.

Make a well in the centre of the dry ingredients, add the yeast mixture and egg yolk then mix to a soft dough. Place the dough in a lightly greased bowl, cover loosely with greased plastic wrap, stand in a warm place for about 45 minutes or until doubled in size.

Make the filling by combining the coconut, egg white, sugar, butter and zest in a small bowl, mix well.

Make the glaze by combining the sugar and boiling water in a small bowl, stir until the sugar is dissolved, stir in the lime juice.

Knead the dough on a lightly floured surface for about 5 minutes or until smooth and elastic. Divide the dough evenly into 6 portions. Roll each portion into a 15cm x 25cm (6in x 10in) rectangle. Spread the coconut filling evenly over each rectangle, leaving a 2cm (¾in) border. Roll up from a short side to form rolls, place alongside each other on the prepared tray. Cover with a clean tea towel then stand in a warm place for about 30 minutes or until well risen.

Bake the rolls in a 200°C (400°F) oven for 8 minutes. Reduce heat to 180°C (350°F), cover with foil if over browning, and bake a further 20 minutes or until well risen and the rolls sound hollow when tapped. Turn out onto a wire rack, brush the hot rolls with glaze, sprinkle with the shredded coconut.

MAKES 6 ROLLS

# Sesame Almond Biscuits

These great tasting biscuits can be found at Vietnamese bakeries – about 3 times the size of these.

90g (3oz) unsalted butter
⅔ cup (165g/5½oz) caster sugar
1 teaspoon grated mandarin or orange zest
1 tablespoon sesame seed paste (tahini)
1 egg
¾ cup (110g/3½oz) plain flour
½ cup (60g/2oz) ground almonds
2 tablespoons sesame seeds, toasted

Beat the butter, sugar and mandarin zest in a bowl until just combined. Add the sesame seed paste and egg, mix well.

Stir in the sifted flour and almonds in 2 batches to form a soft dough that comes away from the sides of the bowl. Wrap the dough in plastic wrap then refrigerate for 30 minutes.

Roll level tablespoons of dough into balls, toss in sesame seeds. Place the balls 4cm (1½in) apart on lightly greased baking trays, flatten slightly.

Bake in a 180°C (350°F) oven for about 12 minutes or until browned. Stand for 3 minutes, loosen with a palette knife then cool on the trays.

MAKES ABOUT 20

# Crusty Pineapple and Cashew Tartlets

These tartlets have a beautiful crisp pastry which melts in the mouth. Be careful when lifting them out of the pans. If you like the taste of ginger, add 1 teaspoon of grated fresh ginger to the coconut cream mixture.

*½ cup (75g/2½oz) plain flour*
*½ cup (75g/2½oz) self-raising flour*
*1 tablespoon icing sugar*
*90g (3oz) unsalted butter, chopped*
*1 egg yolk, lightly beaten*
*1 tablespoon water, approximately*
*2 teaspoons icing sugar, extra*
*2 tablespoons coconut cream*
*1 egg, lightly beaten*
*1½ rings glacé pineapple, finely chopped*
*¼ cup (35g/about 1oz) roasted unsalted cashew nuts, chopped*

Lightly grease a 12-hole shallow round-based tartlet tray or patty pan.

Sift the flours into a bowl, stir in the icing sugar and rub in the butter. Add the egg yolk and enough water to make the dough cling together. Gently knead into a ball, cover with plastic wrap, refrigerate for 30 minutes.

Divide the dough evenly into 12 portions. Roll out each portion on a lightly floured surface until about 3mm (⅛in) thick. Cut into rounds using a 7cm (2¾in) fluted cutter.

Place each round into the tray, lightly prick the bases with a fork. Bake in a 200°C (400°F) oven for about 5 minutes or until lightly browned, cool.

Spoon some combined extra icing sugar, coconut cream and egg into each tartlet, sprinkle with some pineapple and cashew nuts.

Bake the tartlets in a 200°C (400°F) oven for about 10 minutes or until set, cool in the tray.

MAKES 12

# Banana and Pistachio Crescents

These delicate little crescents are not typically Vietnamese but do contain such ingredients as pistachio nuts, bananas and rice wine or rum which give them a Vietnamese flavour.

*1 cup (150g/5oz) plain flour*
*90g (3oz) unsalted butter, chopped*
*1 tablespoon icing sugar*
*1½ tablespoons water, approximately*
*1 egg yolk, lightly beaten*
*2 teaspoons finely chopped pistachio nuts*
FILLING
*2½ tablespoons shelled pistachio nuts, finely chopped*
*2 small bananas, finely chopped*
*1 teaspoon honey*
*1 teaspoon rice wine or rum, optional*

Sift the flour into a bowl, rub in the butter. Add the icing sugar and mix well. Stir in enough water for mixture to cling together and form a soft dough. Cover the dough with plastic wrap, refrigerate for 1 hour.

Make the filling by combining the pistachio nuts, bananas, honey and rice wine in a bowl, mix well.

Divide the dough in half, roll out each half until about 3mm (⅛in) thick. Cut into rounds using a 7cm (2¾in) fluted cutter.

Spoon level teaspoons of the filling onto the centre of each round, brush edges lightly with water then fold the pastry over to enclose the filling. Press firmly to seal the edges. Place the crescents onto a greased baking tray, brush with beaten egg yolk, sprinkle with the chopped pistachio nuts.

Bake the crescents in a 190°C (375°F) oven for about 10 minutes or until lightly browned and crisp. Stand 3 minutes then loosen with a palette knife. Serve warm or cold.

MAKES ABOUT 20

# Banana and Coconut Tart

This tart can be kept for a couple of days in the refrigerator. It is quite simple to make and has a delicious banana and coconut flavour.

*1 x 25cm (10in) square sheet frozen*
*shortcrust pastry, thawed*
*1 cup (250ml/8fl oz) coconut milk*
*¼ cup (50g/1½oz) grated palm sugar or ¼ cup*
*(60g/2oz) brown sugar*
*¼ cup (60ml/2fl oz) coconut cream*
*2 eggs, lightly beaten*
*1 teaspoon grated fresh ginger*
*3 small bananas, chopped*

Place the pastry into a deep 20cm (8in) round flan tin. Ease the pastry into the sides of the tin and trim away the excess. Use the offcuts of pastry to patch the sides, pressing firmly to adhere the edges. Trim away the excess pastry.

Cover the pastry with baking paper then fill with dried beans or rice. Bake in a 200°C (400°F) oven for 10 minutes. Remove the paper and beans then bake for a further 8 minutes. Remove from the oven.

Combine half the coconut milk with the palm sugar in a saucepan then stir over low heat until the sugar is dissolved. Combine with the remaining coconut milk, coconut cream, eggs and ginger in a bowl and mix well. Place the bananas in the base of the pastry case, carefully pour over the coconut milk mixture. Bake in a 180°C (350°F) oven for about 40 minutes or until a knife inserted in the centre comes out clean. Serve the tart warm or cold.

SERVES 6

*LEFT: Banana and Coconut Tart*

# Coconut Pancakes with Mango and Passionfruit

Use a tropical liqueur such as Malibu or, if you prefer, use an orange-flavoured liqueur. The pancakes can be made several hours ahead and reheated just prior to serving.

*1 cup (150g/5oz) self-raising flour*
*¼ cup (20g/⅔oz) coconut, toasted*
*2 tablespoons caster sugar*
*1 egg*
*¾ cup (185ml/6fl oz) milk, approximately*
*2 tablespoons shredded coconut, toasted*
MANGO AND PASSIONFRUIT
*1 large ripe mango*
*2 tablespoons liqueur*
*pulp of 4 passionfruit*

Sift the flour into a bowl, stir in the coconut and the sugar. Lightly beat the egg and milk together, gradually add to the flour mixture, mixing to a smooth thick batter. You may need a little extra milk. Stand the batter for 30 minutes.

Heat a greased frying pan, add 2–3 tablespoons of the batter and cook until bubbles appear on the surface. Turn the pancake over and cook until puffed and lightly browned underneath. Repeat cooking the pancakes with the remaining batter, keeping the pancakes warm if it is close to serving time.

Prepare the Mango and Passionfruit. Chop the mango, purée half the mango in a blender with the liqueur until smooth. Stir in the passionfruit pulp.

Serve the hot pancakes drizzled with the mango purée and topped with the remaining chopped mango and shredded coconut.

SERVES 4

VARIATION
In place of the milk, use coconut milk for a stronger coconut flavour.

# The Essentials

## Red Curry Paste

*4 cloves garlic, crushed*
*1 small onion, chopped*
*3 tablespoons chopped lemon grass*
*2 tablespoons chopped fresh coriander*
*8 red chillies, chopped*
*2 teaspoons galangal powder*
*1 teaspoon shrimp paste*
*1 tablespoon paprika*
*$^1/_4$ cup (60ml/2fl oz) oil*
*1 teaspoon ground coriander*
*1 teaspoon ground cumin*

Process all the ingredients together to make a paste in the food processor.

MAKES ABOUT $^3/_4$ CUP (185ML/6FL OZ)

## Chilli Oil

*$^1/_2$ cup (125ml/4fl oz) oil – preferably peanut oil*
*5 red chillies, chopped*

Heat the oil in a small saucepan until hot. Remove from the heat, add the chillies, being careful the mixture does not bubble over. Stand at room temperature until cool. Strain into a glass jar or small bottle, seal well. It will keep for up to a month.

MAKES $^1/_2$ CUP (125ML/4FL OZ)

## Chilli Lime Sauce

*8 red or green chillies*
*4 cloves garlic, finely chopped*
*$^2/_3$ cup (160ml/5$^1/_2$fl oz) lime juice*
*2 tablespoons fish sauce*
*2 tablespoons chopped fresh coriander*

Process all the ingredients together to make a paste in the food processor.

MAKES ABOUT 1 CUP (250ML/8FL OZ)

## Green Curry Paste

*10 small green chillies, chopped*
*6 green shallots (spring onions), chopped*
*4 cloves garlic, crushed*
*3 tablespoons chopped lemon grass*
*$^1/_4$ cup (60ml/2fl oz) oil*
*$^1/_2$ cup (15g/$^1/_2$oz) chopped fresh coriander*
*2 teaspoons shrimp paste*
*1 teaspoon grated lime zest*
*$^1/_2$ teaspoon ground cumin*
*$^1/_2$ teaspoon ground coriander*

Process all the ingredients together to make a paste in the food processor.

MAKES ABOUT 1 CUP (250ML/8FL OZ)

## Chilli and Peanut Sauce

*$^1/_4$ cup (75g/2$^1/_2$oz) sugar*
*$^1/_3$ cup (80ml/2$^1/_2$fl oz) white vinegar*
*2 red chillies, chopped*
*1 tablespoon chopped unsalted roasted peanuts*
*2 green shallots (spring onions), finely chopped*

Combine the sugar and vinegar in a small saucepan, stir over low heat until the sugar is dissolved. Add the remaining ingredients and cool.

MAKES ABOUT $^1/_2$ CUP (125ML/4FL OZ)

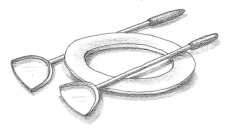

*ABOVE: Clockwise from top right: Red Curry Paste; Chilli and Peanut Sauce; Chilli Lime Sauce*

## Peanut Sauce

*2 teaspoons oil*
*2 cloves garlic, crushed*
*1/2 teaspoon grated fresh ginger*
*2 teaspoons sweet chilli sauce*
*1 tablespoon hoi sin sauce*
*1/3 cup (80ml/2 1/2fl oz) water*
*1 1/2 tablespoons smooth peanut butter*

Heat the oil in a small saucepan, add the garlic and ginger, stir over heat for about 2 minutes or until aromatic. Add the sweet chilli sauce, hoi sin sauce, water and peanut butter, stir until the mixture is smooth, cool.

Make the sauce up to 1 week ahead and store, covered in the refrigerator. If the sauce becomes too thick on standing, add a little water to thin it down.

MAKES ABOUT 1/2 CUP (125ML/4FL OZ)

## Fish Dipping Sauce

*1 1/2 tablespoons boiling water*
*1 tablespoon caster sugar*
*1 small red chilli, seeded and finely chopped*
*2 cloves garlic, crushed*
*1 tablespoon rice vinegar*
*1 1/2 tablespoons lime juice*
*1 1/2 tablespoons fish sauce*

Combine the water and sugar in a small bowl, stir until the sugar has dissolved, cool.

Add the chilli, garlic, vinegar, lime juice and fish sauce to the sugar syrup, mix well.

MAKES ABOUT 1/2 CUP (125ML/4FL OZ)

## Shallot Oil

*1/3 cup (80ml/2 1/2fl oz) oil – preferably peanut oil*
*3 green shallots (spring onions), finely chopped*

Heat the oil in a small saucepan until hot, remove from the heat. Add the green shallots (spring onions), being careful the mixture doesn't bubble over. Stand at room temperature until cool.

Strain the oil into a glass jar or small bottle, seal well. It will keep for up to a month.

MAKES 1/3 CUP (80ML/2 1/2FL OZ)

# Index

## A

Almond sesame biscuits 150
Aromatic beef and aniseed soup 35
Aromatic beef casserole with fennel and daikon 121
Artichoke and potato cakes 94
Aubergines see Eggplant

## B

Baguette, cinnamon sausage 101
Baked chicken strips with ginger and tomato 70
Baked noodles with prawns and broccoli 112
Baked whole fish 105
Bananas
    and coconut tart 153
    crisp, with caramel sauce 147
    and pistachio crescents 151
Barbecued chicken livers and potato scallops 71
Barbecued duck salad 139
Barbecued peppered chicken with chilli sauce 77
Barbecued pineapple with vegetables 92
Barbecued pork
    with spinach 85
    with stir-fried rice 52
Barbecued prawns on sugar cane 28
Bean thread vermicelli with lime, cucumber and orange 54
Beans
    with cauliflower and scallops 143
    and noodle salad 139
    sauce 82
Beef
    and aniseed aromatic soup 35
    aromatic casserole with fennel and daikon 121
    in coconut milk with baby onions 121
    creamy curry 116
    meatball and cucumber soup 38
    minced 117
    omelette scrolls 22
    in peanut sauce 125
    salad 135
    slow-cooked spicy 119
    steaks with slivered mango and vegetables 122
    and sweet potato dry curry 120
    tomato and bamboo with rice 60
Belgian endive see Witlof
Biscuits
    almond sesame 150
    banana and pistachio crescents 151
Braised chicken drumsticks 67
Braised quail eggs and vegetables 94
Broccoli and chilli nutty omelette 91

Brown rice with tofu and ginger 55
Buns, steamed spicy vegetarian 19

## C

Capsicum and eggplant with wonton noodle strips 58
Caramel sauce 147
Carrot, pickled 129
Cashew bags 26
Cellophane noodles and chilli vegetables 48
Char-grilled lamb and eggplant with ginger sauce 122
Char-grilled octopus 110
Chick peas and couscous with herbs and coconut cream 99
Chicken
    and asparagus, stir-fried 67
    baked strips of, with ginger and tomato 70
    barbecued peppered, with chilli sauce 77
    and basil salad 142
    braised drumsticks 67
    and capsicum with rice noodles 54
    with Chinese greens and coconut cream 72
    and coriander rounds 20
    and corn wedges 26
    and crab spring rolls 23
    curry with carrot and parsnip 75
    green curry 66
    grilled lemon grass and chicken 70
    hot and sour soup 39
    marinated, with julienne vegetables 72
    noodle lettuce cups 75
    and rice casserole 61
    and rice noodle soup 34
    scallop and orange salad 134
    shredded, with spicy eggplant 128
    stuffed spatchcocks with nutty cinnamon rice 78
    with Thai seasoning 81
    in tomato sauce, with minted rice 60
Chicken livers
    with chilli 77
    and potato scallops, barbecued 71
Chilli
    and coconut rice 55
    garlic quail with ginger 66
    lime dressing 134
    lime sauce 154
    oil 154
    and peanut sauce 154
    sauce 77

Cinnamon sausage baguette 101
Citrus and ginger fruit 147
Coconut
    and banana tart 153
    and chilli rice 55
    ice cream and mango with lime and ginger 146
    kumara puddings 146
    pancakes with mango and passionfruit 153
    and sultana rolls 150
Coriander pesto 105
Couscous and chick peas with herbs and coconut cream 99
Crab
    and chicken spring rolls 23
    and pork cubes 17
    and prawn cakes 106
Creamy beef curry 116
Crisp bananas with caramel sauce 147
Crisp cashew bags 26
Crisp noodles and alfalfa 62
Crisp tofu in tomato sauce 101
Crusty pineapple and cashew tartlets 151
Cucumber
    grapefruit and sprout salad 132
    pickled 129
Curry
    chicken, with carrot and parsnip 75
    creamy beef 116
    dry beef and sweet potato 120
    eggplant and potato 98
    green chicken 66
    pork and coconut, with noodles and sprouts 62
    pork turnovers 31
    prawns with cucumber and asparagus 106
    spiced pork 84
Curry paste
    green 154
    red 154

## D

Daikon radish, pickled 129
Dipping sauce
    fish 155
    tomato, with vegetable crudités 31
Dry beef and sweet potato curry 120
Duck
    barbecued, salad of 138
    spicy roasted breast rolls 68
Duck, barbecued, salad of 139

**E**

Egg
    see also Omelette; Quail eggs
    thread and tomato soup 35
    and tofu warm salad 91
    vegetable and bean sprout stir-fry 93
Egg noodles
    with basil, coriander and mint 52
    and bean salad 139
    and sprouts with pork and coconut curry 62
    and vegetable stir-fry 44
Eggplant
    and capsicum with wonton noodle strips 58
    and potato curry 98
    salad 138
    spicy, with shredded chicken 128

**F**

Fish
    baked whole 105
    cutlets with piquant vegetables 102
    dipping sauce 155
    fried cakes 17
    grilled cutlets with Thai pesto 105
    salad with mint and beans 135
    steamed whole, with lemon grass and
        chilli 102
    strips and prawns with ginger and herbs 116
Fried noodles 45
Fried rice, southern 51
Fruit
    citrus and ginger 147
    moulds with mango cream 149

**G**

Garlic herb oysters 22
Ginger pork steaks with honey spiced
    onions 88
Glazed pork ribs with capsicum 82
Glazed pumpkin and zucchini 132
Glutinous rice with beans and sesame seeds 49
Grapefruit, sprout and cucumber salad 132
Green beans with cauliflower and scallops 143
Green curry
    chicken 66
    paste 154
Green pawpaw, pork and carrot salad 140
Greens and reds in spicy sauce 138
Greens with chilli and herbs 128
Grilled crab and prawn cakes 106
Grilled fish cutlets with Thai pesto 105
Grilled lemon grass and chilli chicken 70

**H**

Ham soup with rice and yellow mung beans 40
Honey spiced quail 71
Hot and sour chicken soup 39

**I**

Ice cream, coconut, with mango, lime and
    ginger 146

**J**

Jasmine rice
    chilli and coconut 55
    steamed 44
    with tofu and ginger 55

**K**

Kumara
    and coconut cream soup 38
    coconut puddings 146

**L**

Lamb
    and baby onion sticks 30
    char-grilled, with eggplant and ginger
        sauce 122
    with eggplant and tamarind 119
    with lemon grass and cashew nuts 120
    lime and watercress salad 143
    patty salad 130, 136
    roast, with Thai seasoning 117
    rolls with sesame peanut sauce 115
    and spinach with soft rice noodles 61
Lamb's liver with garlic and black pepper 125
Layered pork and mushroom casserole 88
Lemon and dill seafood soup 34
Lemon grass mussels 27
Lettuce cups, chicken noodle 75
Lime and pork patties 25
Liver, lamb's, with garlic and black pepper 125

**M**

Mango
    with coconut ice cream, lime and ginger 146
    with coconut pancakes and passionfruit 153
    cream 149
Marinated chicken with julienne vegetables 72
Marinated tofu with vegetables 98
Meatball and cucumber soup 38
Minced beef, Thai style 117
Minted peanut sauce 89
Minted rice with chicken in tomato sauce 60
Mixed vegetable soup 39
Mussels, lemon grass 27

**N**

Noodles
    see also Egg noodles; Rice noodles; Vermicelli
    and chilli vegetables 48
    crisp, with alfalfa 62
Nutty broccoli and chilli omelette 91

**O**

Octopus
    char-grilled 110
    stir-fried with pickled mustard greens 109
Oil
    chilli 154
    shallot 155
Omelette
    beef scrolls 22
    nutty broccoli and chilli 91

peppered pork rolls 84
    rice and shrimp paste rolls 46
Oven-baked marinated pork fillet 30
Oven-baked spring rolls 27
Oysters, garlic herb 22

**P**

Pancakes
    coconut, with mango and passionfruit 153
    pork and bean sprout 89
Pan-fried fish cakes 17
Pawpaw, pork and carrot salad 140
Peanut
    and chilli sauce 154
    minted sauce 89
    sauce 155
    sesame sauce 115
Peppered pork and omelette rolls 84
Pesto, Thai 105
Pickled carrot, daikon radish or cucumber 129
Pickled vegetables with bacon 129
Pineapple
    barbecued with vegetables 92
    and cashew tartlets 151
Pork
    see also Barbecued pork
    and bean sprout pancakes 89
    chilli, with witlof 16
    cinnamon sausage baguette 101
    with citrus marinade and spinach 86
    and coconut curry with noodles and
        sprouts 62
    and crab cubes 17
    curried turnovers 31
    ginger steaks with honey spiced onions 88
    green pawpaw and carrot salad 140
    and lime patties 25
    and mushroom layered casserole 88
    and noodle stuffed squid 109
    and omelette rolls 84
    oven-baked marinated fillet 30
    prawns and vegetables with steamed rice 57
    soup with rice and yellow mung beans 40
    spiced curry 84
    steamed patties with minted peanut sauce 89
    stir-fried, with red curry paste 86
    and tofu stack with bean sauce 82
Pork ribs
    glazed, with capsicum 82
    spicy 85
Potato
    and artichoke cakes 94
    and eggplant curry 98
    scallops and chicken livers, barbecued 71
Prawns
    barbecued, on sugar cane 28
    and broccoli with baked noodles 112
    and crab cakes 106
    curried, with cucumber and asparagus 106
    and fish strips with ginger and herbs 116

with leeks in fish sauce 19
with lemon grass and chilli 110
pork and vegetables with steamed rice 57
sesame toasts 16
skewered saté 25
wonton soup 36
Puddings, kumara coconut 146
Pumpkin and zucchini, glazed 132

**Q**
Quail
chilli garlic, with ginger 66
roasted honey spiced 71
Quail eggs braised with vegetables 94

**R**
Red curry paste 154
Rice
see also Jasmine rice; Steamed rice
balls 45
with beef, tomato and bamboo 60
and chicken casserole 61
glutinous, with beans and sesame
seeds 49
minted, with chicken in tomato sauce 60
and shrimp paste omelette rolls 46
southern fried 51
sticky dessert with ginger syrup 149
stir-fried, with barbecued pork 52
Rice noodles
baked, with prawns and broccoli 112
with chicken and capsicum 54
and chicken soup 34
fried 45
with lamb and spinach 61
peanut and spinach stir-fry 99
and seafood toss 48
in Thai sauce 51
Rice vermicelli, crisp, with alfalfa 62
Roast lamb with Thai seasoning 117
Roasted honey spiced quail 71

**S**
Salad
barbecued duck 139
cellophane noodles and chilli vegetables 48
chicken, scallop and orange 134
chicken and basil 142
eggplant 138
fish, with mint and beans 135
grapefruit, sprout and cucumber 132
green pawpaw, pork and carrot 140
lamb, lime and watercress 143
lamb patty 130, 136
noodle and bean 139
Thai beef 135
vegetable, with chilli lime dressing 134
warm egg and tofu 91
Saté prawns 25

Sauce
bean 82
caramel 147
chilli 77
chilli and peanut 154
chilli lime 154
minted peanut 89
peanut 155
sesame peanut 115
Sausage baguette 101
Scallops
chicken and orange salad 134
with green beans and cauliflower 143
Seafood
and fresh rice noodle toss 48
with herbs, chilli and garlic 112
lemon and dill soup 34
Sesame
almond biscuits 150
lamb and baby onion sticks 30
peanut sauce 115
prawn toasts 16
Shallot oil 155
Skewered saté prawns 25
Slow-cooked spicy beef 119
Smoked pork soup with rice and yellow mung
beans 40
Soup
aromatic beef and aniseed 35
beef meatball and cucumber 38
chicken and rice noodle 34
hot and sour chicken 39
kumara and coconut cream 38
lemon and dill seafood 34
mixed vegetable 39
prawn wonton 36
smoked pork, with rice and yellow mung
beans 40
tomato and egg thread 35
Southern fried rice 51
Spatchcocks, stuffed, with nutty cinnamon rice 78
Spiced pork curry 84
Spicy eggplant with shredded chicken 128
Spicy pork ribs 85
Spicy roasted duck breast rolls 68
Spinach, rice noodle and peanut stir-fry 99
Spring rolls
chicken and crab 23
oven-baked 27
tofu and vegetable, with spicy dressing 96
Sprout, grapefruit and cucumber salad 132
Squid, stuffed, and pork noodle 109
Steamed pork patties with minted peanut
sauce 89
Steamed rice 49
jasmine 44
with pork, prawns and vegetables 57

Steamed spicy vegetarian buns 19
Steamed whole fish with lemon grass and
chilli 102
Sticky rice dessert with ginger syrup 149
Stir-fried chicken and asparagus 67
Stir-fried octopus with pickled mustard
greens 109
Stir-fried pork with curry paste 86
Stir-fried rice with barbecued pork 52
Stuffed spatchcocks with nutty cinnamon rice 78
Sweet potato see Kumara

**T**
Tart
banana and coconut 153
crusty pineapple and cashew 151
Tofu
with brown rice and ginger 55
crisp, in tomato sauce 101
and egg warm salad 91
marinated, with vegetables 98
and pork stack with bean sauce 82
steamed spicy vegetarian buns 19
and vegetable fresh spring rolls with spicy
dressing 96
Tomatoes
dip with vegetable crudités 31
and egg thread soup 35
stuffed with rice and mushrooms 92
Tropical fruit moulds with mango cream 149

**V**
Vegetables
bean sprout and egg strip stir-fry 93
and chilli cellophane noodles 48
crudités with tomato dip 31
and egg noodle stir-fry 44
greens and reds in spicy sauce 138
greens with chilli and herbs 128
pickled, with bacon 129
with pineapple, barbecued 92
platter with a dipping sauce 142
salad with chilli lime dressing 134
soup 39
steamed buns 19
stir-fry 138
Vermicelli
crisp, with alfalfa 62
with lime, cucumber and orange 54

**W**
Warm salad of egg and tofu 91
Witlof with chilli pork 16
Wonton
noodle strips with eggplant and capsicum 58
prawn soup 36

**Z**
Zucchini and pumpkin, glazed 132